The
Art
of
Meditation

The
Art
of
Meditation

Bishop Joseph Hall

Sovereign Grace Publishers, Inc.
P.O. Box 4998
Lafayette, IN 47903
Http://www.SovGracePub.com

Printed In the United States of America
By Lightning Source, Inc.

CONTENTS.

THE ART OF DIVINE MEDITATION

I suppose that it is profitable, rather than bold, for me to endeavor to teach the art of meditation. It is as heavenly a business as any that belongs to either men or Christians. And it is such a heavenly business as does unspeakably benefit the soul.

For it is by meditation that we ransack our deep and false hearts, find out our secret enemies, come to grips with them, expel them, and arm ourselves against their re-entrance. By meditation we make use of all good means, fit ourselves for all good duties. By meditation we see our weaknesses, obtain redress, prevent temptations, cheer up our loneliness, temper our occasions of delight, get more light unto our knowledge, add more heat to our affections, put more life into our devotions.

It is only by meditation that we are able to be strangers upon the earth (as we are commanded to be), and by this we are brought to a right estimation of all earthly things, finally into a sweet enjoyment of invisible comforts. It is by meditation that we see our Saviour, as Stephen did; we talk with God, as Moses did; we are ravished into Paradise, with blessed Paul, seeing that Heaven that we shall be so loath to leave, which things we cannot utter.

Meditation alone is the remedy for security and worldliness. It is the pastime of saints, the ladder to Heaven; in short, it is the best way to improve Christianity. Learn it, if you can. Neglect it if you so desire, but he who does so shall never find joy—neither in God, nor in himself. And though some of old have appropriated this duty to themselves (confining it within their cells, professing nothing but contemplation), claiming their immunity from those cares which accompany an active life, might have the best leisure for meditation, yet I deem it an envious wrong to conceal meditation from many, for its benefit may be universal. There is no man who is so taken up with action that he does not at some time have a free mind. And no reasonable mind is so simple as not to be able to better itself by secret thoughts. Those who have but little stock need best to know the rules of thrift.

Surely divine meditation is nothing else but a bending of the mind upon some spiritual object, through different forms of discourse, until our thoughts come to an issue. And this must either be unpremeditated, occasioned by outward occurrences offered to the mind; or else it must be deliberate, wrought out of our own heart. And if it is deliberate, then it is either in matter of knowledge (for finding out some hidden truth, or overcoming some heresy by profound traversing of reason); or it is in matter of affection (for kindling our love toward God). The former of these last two we will send to the schools, to the masters of controversies, and we will search for the latter. For heavenly affection is of much larger use, something no Christian can reject as unnecessary or over-difficult. For every Christian needs fire put to his affections, and weaker judgments are no less capable of this divine heat— for it comes from faith, not from reason.

One says, and I believe him, that God's school is more about affection than understanding. Both lessons are needful, very profitable, but in this age that of affection more so. For there are some who have much zeal, little knowledge, but there are more that have much knowledge without zeal. Now he that has much skill, but no affection, may do good to others by giving information for judgment—but he shall never get any thanks either from his own heart or from God (who does not usually cast away His love on those who know Him but do not love Him).

REGARDING EXTEMPORARY MEDITATION

Of extemporary mediation there may be much use, but no rule. This is because our conceits vary according to the infinite multitude of objects, and their various ways of offering themselves to the mind, and also because of the suddenness of this act. Man is placed on this stage of the world to view the manifold natures and actions of the creation, but not to view them idly, without usefulness to him, as they view him. God made all these for man, and He made man for His own sake. Both of these purposes would be lost if man should let the creatures pass carelessly by him, being seen but not thought upon. If man does not benefit from what he sees, it is the same as if he were blind or brutish. Which is why Solomon sends the sluggard to school to the ant, and it is the reason our Saviour sends the distrustful to the lily of the field.

This is the kind of meditation pursued by the divine psalmist, who upon viewing the glorious frame of the heavens was led to wonder at the merciful respect God had toward so lowly a creature as man. In the same way our Saviour took occasion from the water brought up solemnly to the altar, from the well of Shiloh, on the day of the great Hosannah, to meditate and discourse of the Water of Life. So holy and sweet Augustine took occasion from the water course near his lodging, running among the pebbles silently, then murmuring, then shrilly, to enter into the thought and discourse of that excellent order which God has settled in all these inferior things. So that learned and heavenly soul, the late Mr. Estye, upon occasion of hearing some sweet, comforting music, was at that time carried up to the time when he would enter into his rest, saying, not without some passion, O what music must there be in

Heaven! Thoughts of this kind are not only lawful, but so fitting that we cannot omit them without being charged with neglect of God, his creatures, and ourselves. The creatures are half lost if we only use them, not learning something from them. God is wronged if His creatures are unregarded. Most of all, we wrong ourselves if we read this great volume, the book of creation, and take out of it no lessons for our instruction.

CAUTIONS REGARDING EXTEMPORARY MEDITATIONS

Yet in such things, we must be cautious lest our meditations be too farfetched, lest they savor too much of superstition. I call those farfetched which do not have a fitting and easy resemblance to the matter from which they are raised. In that case our thoughts would prove loose and heartless, making no memorable impression upon the mind. It would be superstitious when we choose those grounds of meditation which are forbidden us, or when we employ our own devices to a use about their reach—for out of our own pleasure we may make them not only steps toward God but parts of the worship of God. In both of these cases our meditations degenerate and grow perilous to the soul. Add to this the fact that the mind must not be surfeited with too frequent repetition of the same thought, which at last breeds a weariness within ourselves, and a displeasure for that knowledge which at first promised much delight. Our nature is too ready to abuse familiarity of any kind. For meditations, like medicines, must not have overordinary use. God has not starved us for matter for our meditations, having given us the scope of the whole world, so that there is no creature, no event, no action, no speech which may not afford us new matter for meditation.

It is said of fine wits that they can make use of anything, so we may as truly affirm this of the Christian heart. Travelers in a foreign country make every sight a lesson, so we ought to do in this pilgrimage of ours. Do you see the heavens rolling above your head in a constant and unmovable motion, the air full of the bottles of rain, the fleecy snow, the sea under one uniform face, full of strange and monstrous shapes? Do you see the earth so adorned with every variety of plant, so much so that you cannot avoid treading upon one at every step? Do you see the store of creatures that fly above the earth, walk upon it, living in it? Idle truant! Do you learn nothing from these things? Have you read these capital letters out of God's book for so long without being able to spell one word. The animals see these same things, perhaps with clearer and better eyes than yours. If your inward eyes do not see their use, as well as your bodily eyes see their shape, I do not know which (animals or men) can be said to be more reasonable, or less brutish.

CONCERNING DELIBERATE MEDITATION

Our chief concern here is with deliberate meditation. This may be guided and furthered by precepts, part of which may be the labors of others and part the work of the plainest mistress: Experience. Good order would require that we first look at the qualities of the person fit for meditation, then the circumstances, the manner, and the procedure.

QUALIFICATIONS OF THE MEDITATOR

The hill of meditation may not be climbed with a profane foot. As when the Law was delivered to Israel, so here, no beast may touch God's mountain lest he die. Only the pure of heart have a promise that they may see God. Sin dims and dazzles the eye, so much so that it cannot behold spiritual things. The guard of heavenly soldiers were all around Elisha's servant (2 Kings 6:17), but he did not see them because of the scales of his infidelity.

1. Therefore, first, the soul must be purged before it can profitably meditate.

As in days of old they usually would search for and thrust out malefactors from the presence before they went to sacrifice, so must we search for our sins and thrust them out before we offer our thoughts to God. First, David said, I will wash my hands in innocence, then I will go about Thy altar. That worthy chancellor of Paris made the first stair of his ladder of contemplation to be Humble Repentance. The cloth that is white (the color of purity) is the cloth that is capable of taking any dye. A black cloth takes the color of no other. It is not that an absolute perfection (which is true of none, and if it were it would exclude all need for meditation) is required, but rather an honest sincerity of heart. We must not willingly sin, we must willingly repent when we have sinned—and if you find these in yourself, you need not fear that any weakness will bar you from meditation. He who pleads this excuse is like some simple man who is half dead with cold yet refuses to come near the fire because he does not have heat enough.

2. The mind must be free from worldly thoughts.

If any soul hopes to profit by meditation, he must not allow himself to be entangled with the world. This would be the same as coming to God's holy bush with our shoes on our feet (Exod. 3). A bird with her feathers limed is unable to fly as she once did. So are we when our thoughts are glued together by the world, we cannot soar up to Heaven via meditation. James and John must leave their nets if they are to follow Christ; Elisha must leave his oxen before he can follow a prophet. The mind that ascends this mountain of meditation must be free and light, else it will not overcome this height, this steepness. Cares are a heavy load. These must be laid down at the bottom of this mountain, if we ever are to reach the top. You may be loaded down with household cares, perhaps public affairs, and I do not tell you to cast them away. These have their time, to omit them would be impiety. I tell you to lay them down at your closet door when you attempt this work of meditation. If you let them in with you, you shall find them troublesome companions, always distracting you from your errand. If you desire to think of Heaven, your barn gets in your way. It may be your accounts, or a trip which you are about to take. While you think of these things, you will think of nothing. While your mind is going many ways, it will go nowhere. As when a crowd presses forward to go through but one door, no one goes through. So when a variety of thoughts tumble tumultuously through the mind, each proves a bar to the others, all are a hindrance to him who entertains such thoughts.

3. The meditator must be constant.

As our client of meditation must both be pure and free from care, so he also must be constant in continuing it. This constancy must be in both time and matter. There must be a set course and a set hour reserved for this work, and the prosecution of it must be unwearied once it is begun. Those that meditate by snatches and uncertain fits (meditating only when all other work forsakes them, or when good motions are thrust upon them by necessity) may never expect to reach any perfection in meditation. For any feeble beginnings of lukewarm grace which may be wrought in them by one fit of serious meditation shall soon be extinguished by intermitting time. They shall perish. This one day's meal, though large and liberal, does not strengthen you for tomorrow. The body will languish if there is not a daily supply of food. So you must feed your soul by meditation. Then set your hours and keep them, do not yield to an easy distraction. There is no difficulty in this except in the beginning. Practice shall make it not only easy, it shall make it a delight.

Your companion may offer to entertain you, or some unexpected business may offer to interrupt you. There is never any good work but what there shall be some hindrance. Either you must break through the hindrances, or, in the event that you will suffer loss, or if importunity demands, you must repay yourself the time that was unseasonably borrowed from meditation. Repay your omitted hours with the double labors of another day, for you shall find that deferring breeds an indisposition to good (besides your loss for the omitted day). What was before pleasant to you, being omitted, tomorrow grows harsh, the next day it is unnecessary, and afterward it becomes odious. Today you can, but you will not. Tomorrow you could, but you do not want to. The next day you neither will nor can bend your mind on these thoughts. So I have seen friends who neglect this duty grow excessive. When they become excessive, then they become alienated. Once they become alienated, they then begin to utter defiance.

Surely those whose trade is divinity should never omit a day without his time of meditation. Those who are in secular life should not omit many, remembering that they have a common calling in the service of Christianity, as well as a special vocation in the world. The first of these is more noble and important, and so it may justly challenge us to frequent and diligent service.

This constancy in regard to meditation not only requires that you be constant in course and in time, but also in the same train of thought. Your mind should dwell upon the same thought without flitting, without weariness, until it has attained to some issue of spiritual profit. Otherwise it attempts much but effects nothing. What does it avail to knock at the door of the heart, if we leave before we have an answer? Are we going to be any more fervent if we merely pass hastily along beside the heart, not stopping by it? Those damsels who too lightly give their love, who betroth themselves upon first sight, are not much thought of. But those who require long and earnest solicitation, these we deem of much worth. He who thinks that grace is easily won deceives himself. Grace will not yield to us without much pleading and importunity.

Not that we require perpetuity in this labor of meditation, for human frailty could never bear such great toil. Nothing under Heaven is capable of a continual motion without complaint. It is fairly enough for the glorified spirits above to be ever thinking and never weary. The mind of man is of a strange metal, if it is not used, it rusts. If it is used hardly, it breaks. And, briefly, it is more apt to be dulled than satisfied with a continued meditation. That is why some of the ancient monks proved so excellent in this divine business, because they intermixed bodily labor with their contemplations. Whereas the monks and priests of this day, caging themselves away from the world, spend themselves wholly upon their beads and crucifix, pretending to do nothing else but meditate— these have cold hearts towards God and show the world nothing but a dull shadow of devotion. For even if the thoughts of these latter ones were as divine as they are superstitious, yet being without change, bent upon the same discourse, the mind must necessarily grow weary, the thoughts remiss and languishing, the objects tedious. While the others had refreshed themselves with this wise variety, employing their hands while they called off their minds, thus gaining both enough for the body and for the soul, more so than if they had all the while been busied with meditation.

Besides, the excellency of the object prevents this assiduity of meditation. For the object which we seek to know is so glorious it is like the sun, which will allow an eye to be cast upon it for a little while, but it will not permit a steady gazing. So he who attempts to do so, he loses both his hope and his wits. If we hold with blessed Monica that such cogitations are the food of the mind, yet even the mind also has her satiety and may surfeit from too much. Therefore, it is sufficient for us to persevere in our meditation, without any such affectation of perpetuity, and to leave without a light fickleness. We should not make our hour-glass the judge of our constancy, but some competent increase in our devotion. For we know (as is the case with Heaven) that our purpose, to obtain grace, will be little availed if we only begin well, having no perseverance. And it is well to consider that the soul of man is not always in the same disposition, but it sometimes is longer in settling, because of some unquietness, or because of a distraction. It is sometimes heavier, sometimes more active and nimble to dispatch. Persist, therefore, and prevail. Persist until you have prevailed, so that which you began with difficulty may end in comfort.

CONCERNING THE CIRCUMSTANCES OF MEDITATION

From the qualities of the person, we descend toward the action itself. Here we meet with those circumstances which are necessary for our predisposition to the work of meditation: Place, Time, and Position.

THE PLACE FOR MEDITATION

A solitary place is best for meditation. If you desire to talk profitably with yourself, retire from others. So Jesus meditates alone in the Mount, Isaac in the fields, John the Baptist in the desert, David upon his bed, Chrysostom in the bath. Each was in a different place, but all were solitary. There is no place free from God, no place to which He is more tied. One finds his closet the most convenient, his eyes being limited by the known walls, the mind being called from a wandering abroad. Another finds his soul more free when it beholds the heaven above and about him. It does not matter so long as we are solitary and silent. It was a witty and divine saying of Bernard, that the Spouse of the soul, even Christ Jesus, is bashful, not willingly coming to His bride in the presence of a multitude. And so we find that sweet invitation in Solomon's Song, "Come My wellbeloved, let us go forth into the fields, let us lodge in the villages. Let us go up early to the vines, let us see if the vine flourishes, if it has disclosed the first grape, whether the pomegranates blossom, there I will give you My love."

Therefore abandon all worldly society, so that you may change it for the company of God and His angels. I say, from the world, not only outwardly, but inwardly also. There are many who sequester themselves from the visible company of men, but they still carry the world within them. They are alone in body, but they are haunted by a throng of imaginations. As it was with Jerome, who in the wildest desert found himself too often (in his thoughts) among the dances of the Roman women. This company is worse than the other. For it is possible for some men to have a solitary mind in the midst of a market, more so than for such a man to be so disposed in a wilderness. A world of people on the outside, or thoughts peopled with the world on the inside, either are enemies to meditation.

A great master in this art has said that there are three things requisite to this business, Secrecy, Silence, Rest. Secrecy excludes company, Silence excludes noise, Rest excludes motion. It is beyond expression, how subject we are to distraction. The threefold cords of judgment will not easily draw us from sensual delights, but our spiritual pleasures are easily hindered. Therefore choose that place which will admit the fewest occasions of withdrawing your soul from good thoughts. Even a change of places is apt to prejudice our success. I do not know how it happens, but we find God nearer to us in the place where we have been accustomed to meet with Him. It is not that His presence is confined to one place above others, but that our thoughts are through custom more easily gathered to the place where we have been accustomed to meet with Him.

THE TIME OF MEDITATION

God is not bound to hours, nor does the contrary disposition of men agree in one choice of opportunities. Some find the golden hours of the morning to be best for meditation, when the body is newly raised, when it is calmed by rest, when the soul has not yet had any alienation caused by outward things. Others find it best to learn wisdom in the night, hoping with Job that their bed will bring them comfort in their meditation. Then all other things are still, then, wearied with these earthly cares, we may out of contempt for these things grow into a greater desire for and love of heavenly things. I have always found Isaac's time best, who went out in the evening to meditate. No precept, no practice of others can prescribe to us in this circumstance. It shall be enough that we first set ourselves a time, that we set apart that time which is most apt for this service. No time is unfit, every day is a good day for this work, but especially God's day. No day is barren of grace to the searcher of it, none are as fruitful as God's day, which God has sanctified to Himself, and which we are to sanctify to God. The plentiful instruction of that day stirs you up to this action, fills you with matter of thought, and the zeal of your public service warms your heart to this other business of devotion. No manna fell to the Israelites on their Sabbath, our spiritual manna falls on ours most frequently. If you desire a full soul, gather as it falls, gather it by hearing, reading, meditation. Spiritual idleness is a fault, no less so than bodily idleness.

THE POSITION FOR MEDITATION

There is just as much variety in the position of the body, the composedness of which is of great advantage to this exercise. In our speech to God we do not always observe the same position—sometimes we fall groveling on our faces; sometimes we bow our knees; sometimes we stand on our feet; sometimes we lift up our hands; sometimes we cast down our eyes. God is a Spirit who is a close observer of the disposition of the soul, therefore He is not so scrupulous in observing the body. He does not require that the gesture of the body be uniform, but it must be reverent.

It is no marvel, though, that all our teachers of meditation have commended various positions of the body, according to their own disposition and practice. One sitting with the face turned toward heaven follows the precept of the philosopher who taught him that the mind gathers wisdom by sitting and resting. Another leans toward the left side so that the heart may be more quiet. A third stands with his eyes lifted up to Heaven, but shut for fear of distractions. But of all others, I think that Isaac's choice was best, who meditated walking. In this let every man be his own master. But we must use that frame of body which will testify reverence and which will in some cases stir up further devotion. Also the position of the body must be varied according to the matter of our meditation. If we are thinking of our sins, Ahab's soft pace, the publican's dejected eyes, his hand beating upon his breast, are more fitting. If we meditate of the joys of Heaven, Steven's countenance fixed above, David's hands lifted up on high, are most fitting. In all, the body should be the instrument and slave of the soul, following the affections of it. And truly our devotion is best when the body is commanded to service by the spirit, not being allowed to go before it and by forwardness to provoke its master to follow.

CONCERNING THE MATTER AND SUBJECT OF MEDITATION

The matter and subject of meditation must be divine and spiritual, not evil, not worldly. O the carnal and unprofitable thoughts of men! We all meditate. One meditates how to do evil to others; another how to do some earthly good for himself. Another meditates to his own hurt, thinking to do himself good by accomplishing his lewd desires (the fulfilling of which will prove a bane to his soul). He meditates how he may sin unseen and go to hell with the least noise in the world. Perhaps some better minds bend their thoughts upon the search of natural things, the motions of every heaven and every star, the reason and course of the ebbing and flowing of the sea, etc. Perhaps some meditate upon the various forms of government, the rules of state filling up their busy heads. While desiring to be acquainted with the whole world they are strangers at home. While they seek to know all other things, they remain ignorant of themselves. The God that made them, the vileness of their nature, the danger of their sins, the multitude of their imperfections, the Saviour that bought them, the Heaven that He bought for them, are in the meantime as unknown, as unregarded as if they were not. So foolish children spend their time and labor, turning over leaves to hunt for painted babes, not at all respecting the solid matter under their hands. We fools, when will we be wise? When will we turn our eyes from vanity and, with that sweet singer of Israel, make God's statute our song, and meditation in the house of God our pilgrimage?

Earthly things offer themselves with importunity. We must seek after heavenly things with importunity. If the things of the world were not of such little value, they would not be so forward. And since they are so forward, they do not need any meditation to solicit them. But by the difficulty encountered in entreating spiritual things we know that they are more precious and worthier of our endeavor. So, then, we cannot go amiss as long as we keep ourselves in the track of divinity. While the soul is taken up with thoughts of the Deity in His essence, His attributes, His justice, His power, His wisdom, His mercy, His truth, or of His works (in the creation, preservation, government of all things,) we cannot go astray. We can say with the Psalmist, "I will meditate of the beauty of Thy glorious majesty and Thy wonderful works." These matters of divinity are most directly in our way and best fitting the exercise of meditation, and we should meditate upon those which most of all work compunction in the heart, those which most stir us up to devotion.

The best kind of meditations are those concerning Christ Jesus our Mediator, His incarnation, miracles, life, death, burial, resurrection, ascension, intercession, the benefit of our redemption, the certainty of our election, the graces and proceeding of our sanctification, our glorious estate in paradise which was lost by our first parents, our present vileness, our inclination to sin, our many actual offences, the temptations and deceptions of evil angels, the use of the sacraments, nature and practice of faith and repentance, the miseries of our life, the frailty of it, the certainty of our death, the glory of God's saints above, the terrifying aspect of judgment, the terrors of hell, and the rest of this kind. It is well to have variety in our meditations, for even the strongest stomach does not always delight in one dish. Yet we should change so that our choice may be free from wildness and inconstancy.

THE ENTRANCE INTO MEDITATION—PRAYER

A fine building must show some magnificence in the gate. And great men have ushers to go before them to command reverence and passage. Even the poets of old would implore the aid of their gods before composing their ballads. And the heathen Romans would not enter upon any public business without solemn supplication for good success. How much less should a Christian dare to undertake a spiritual work of great importance (as is meditation) without craving the assistance of his God? To do so is no less than to profess his ability to do well without God's permission. When we think evil, it is from ourselves. When we think good, it is from God. As prayer is our conversation with God, so is each good meditation (according to Bernard) God's conversation with us. The heart must speak to God, so that God may speak to it. Prayer and meditation, then, are two loving twins—if you separate the one, the other languishes.

Prayer makes way for meditation. Meditation gives matter, strength and life to our prayers. By these all other things are sanctified to us and we are sanctified to all holy things. This is the royal servant to perfume and dress our souls, so that they may be fit to converse with the King of Heaven.

But the prayer that leads to meditation need not be long. For that is not intended to be the principal business here. It is but an introduction to another business, nothing else but the gate to the building of meditation. The matter of the prayer shall be directed to the end that our meditation may be guided aright and blessed. It is to ask that our judgment may be enlightened, our thoughts quickened, our wills rectified, our affections whetted for heavenly things, our hearts enlarged toward God, our devotion kindled, and that all distractions may be avoided. In this way we may hope to find our corruptions abated, our graces brought to life, our souls and lives in every way bettered by this exercise.

THE ENTRANCE INTO MEDITATION—CHOICE OF THEME

After the common entrance of prayer, the more particular and proper entrance is to be made—in which the mind recollects and makes choice of the theme or matter on which it will bestow itself for the present. It must settle upon that which it has chosen, then, by conducting an inward questioning within our hearts: "What shall we think upon today?" The unprofitable, the inexpedient, must be rejected. The soul, like some noble hawk, must let the crows and larks pass, not taking the worthless birds that cross her path, but she must light upon a bird of value, one worthy of her flight. Let the soul muse in this way:

"What, O Soul, will you muse upon? You see how little it brings you to wander and rove about in uncertainty. You find how little favor there is in these earthly things, by which you have wearied yourself. Do not, like Martha, trouble yourself any longer with the many and needless thoughts of the world. Only heavenly things can give you comfort. Up then, my soul, mind those things that are above! from which you have come. What could be better than to meditate on the life and glory of God's saints? You will never find a worthier employment than to think upon the estate which you shall one day possess, which you now desire."

THE PROCEEDING OF MEDITATION

Our meditation must proceed in due order, not with troubled mind. not contrary to nature, reason or common sense. It begins in the understanding, it ends in the affections. It begins in the brain, it descends to the heart. It begins on earth, it ascends to Heaven--not suddenly, but by certain steps and degrees until we come to the highest.

A METHOD REJECTED

There is a subtle scale of meditation which is admired by some professors of this art. In fact they far prefer this method to the best directions of Origen, Augustine, Bernard, Hugo, Bonaventure, and whoever has been reputed to be of great perfection in this skill.

Lest I should seem to defraud my reader through envy, I will willingly set forth the several stairs of this method. And though I fear it will scar him rather with the danger of obscuring of his thoughts, yet, lest any man complain of an unknown loss, I shall find room for that which I hold to be too knotty for my text:

THE SCALE OF MEDITATION BY AN ANCIENT UNKNOWN AUTHOR

1. The Question: What I think, or, What I should think.
2. The Exclusion: A repelling of what I should not think.
3. The Choice: What is most necessary: expedient, fitting?
4. The Consideration: An actual thinking upon the matter chosen.
5. The Deliberation: A redoubled consideration, til it is known.
6. Attention: A fixed, earnest reflection by which it is fastened in the mind.
7. Explanation: A clearing of the thing considered by similitudes.
8. Discussion: An extending of the thing considered to other points, in which all questions or doubts are discussed.
9. Distinction: An estimation of the worth of the thing handled.

10. Causation: A confirmation of the estimation thus made.
11. Rumination: A sad and serious meditation upon all the former, until it may work on the affections. From this point on to the degrees of affection.

WHY THIS METHOD IS REJECTED

I do not doubt that an ordinary reader will see at least a double fault in this: Darkness and coincidence. They are too obscurely delivered, and many of them fall into other points, thus some superfluity. For this part, then, concerning the understanding, I would rather require only a deep and firm consideration of the thing propounded. This shall be done if we follow it in our discourse through all the principal places which natural reason will afford us. In this let no man plead ignorance, or fear difficulty, for we are all born logicians up to this point. It is not so much skill that we need in this, but industry. And in the course of this consideration we must not be too curious, we must not make such a precise search for every place and argument, as if we were not to omit any (racking the imagination to bring all in). For the mind, if it is let loose and without rule, will rove to no purpose--and contrariwise, if it is too much fettered with the chains of strict regularity, it does not move at all.

FOREWARNING TO THE MEDITATOR

Before I enter into my treatment, I want to forewarn my reader concerning this first part, which is in the understanding. First, I do not desire to bind every man to the same uniform proceeding. Practice and custom may have taught you other courses more familiar, yet not less direct. Therefore, if you can work in your hearts as deep an apprehension of the matter meditated, that it may duly stir your affections, then that is all that is required.

Secondly, if you apply yourself to this direction, do not think that you are necessarily tied to the following of all these logical steps which shall be set forth in our treatise, if such following should make your meditation lame and imperfect. For there are some themes which will not bear all these steps. For example, when we meditate of God, there is no place for Causes, or for Comparisons. Other themes yield these with such difficulty that the search for them may interrupt the chief work intended. It will be sufficient if you take the most pregnant, the most voluntary ones.

Thirdly, when we make this arrangement in the places following, you must not rack your minds too much with the inquiry thereof. (For example, if meditating of sin, I cannot readily meet with the material and formal causes, nor the appendances.) To do so would be to strive more for logic than for devotion. But with not too much disturbance of our thoughts, quietly pass over to the next. If we break our teeth with the shell, we shall find small pleasure in the kernel.

Now, since I fear that this part of my discourse shall be perplexing to the unlearned reader, I will in this whole process back up my rule with its example. So what may be obscure in the one may by the other be explained. And the same steps which he sees me take, he may likewise tread in any other theme.

THE RECOMMENDED METHOD OF MEDITATION—RULE ONE

First, it is best to seriously consider the thing on which we are meditating:

"What then, O my soul, is the life of the saints? Who are the saints? Are they not the ones who, though weak in holiness upon earth, are perfectly holy above? Are they not the ones who even on earth are perfectly holy in their Saviour, who now are holy in themselves? What is their life but that blessed estate above, in which their glorified soul has full fruition in God?

RULE TWO

Some easy and voluntary division must be made, by which our thoughts may have more room made for them, that our proceeding may be more distinct:

"There is a life of nature, when the soul dwells in the body to inform the earthly burden. There is a life of grace, when the Spirit of God dwells in you. There is a life of glory, when the body is united to the soul and both are united to God—or when, in the meantime, the soul being separated from the body, there is an enjoying of God by the soul alone.

"This life of yours, then, has its ages, has its elevations—for it is but born when you pass out of your body and change this earthly house for a heavenly one. It enters into its full vigor when, at the day of resurrection, you resume your companionship with the body, when the body shall be like you, like your Saviour, immortal and glorious. In this life there may be degrees, but there can be no imperfections. Some may be like the sky, some like the stars, but all shall shine. Some may sit at their Saviour's right hand, others at His left, yet all shall be blessed. If some vessels hold more, all shall be full. None shall complain that they lack, none shall envy him that has more."

RULE THREE

There must be a consideration of the causes. For our most perfect understanding, in order to lay ground for exercising our affections, we must think our way through those principal places, those heads of reason, which nature has taught every man. And this is necessary for our knowledge and for our amplification:

"What is the cause of eternal life? From where does it come? It comes only from Him who alone is eternal, from Him who is the only fountain of life, yea, who is life itself. Who but the God who gave us temporal life could also give us eternal life? The Father gives it, the Son merits it, the Holy Spirit seals and applies it. Therefore, O my soul, expect it only from Him who free election gave you the first title to it, to be purchased by the blood of your Saviour. For you shall not be happy because He foresaw that you would be good. But you are good because He has ordained that you should be happy. He has ordained you to life. He has given you a Saviour to give life to you, faith by which you may attain to this Saviour, His word by which you may gain this faith. What is there that is not His? And yet it is not His so simply that it is without you. It is indeed without your merit, but it is not without your act. Your life on earth is by His blessing, yet it is by use of bread. Your life above is by His mercy, but it is by exercise of faith here below which apprehends the Author of your life. And just as He will not save you without your faith, so you can never have faith without His gift. Then look up to Him, O my soul, as the Author and Finisher of your salvation. And while you magnify the Author, be ravished with the glory of His work, which far surpasses both the tongue of angels and the heart of man. There can be no good thing which is not there. How can they lack water if they have the spring? Where God is enjoyed, in whom all good things are, what good can be lacking? What perfection of bliss must be there, where all goodness meets and is united! "In Thy presence is fullness of joy, and at Thy right hand are pleasures forevermore."

O blessed reflection of Glory! We see there as we are seen. In that we are seen, it is our glory. In that we see, it is God's glory. That is why He glorifies us, that our glory should be His. How worthy art Thou, O Lord, that through us Thou shouldest look at Thyself!"

RULE FOUR

The fruits and effects should be considered. This affords much feeling, copious matter for our meditation. In this it is best, however, to seek for the chief fruits and effects, rather than all:

"It is no marvel, then, if unspeakable joy proceeds from this unspeakable glory. And from this joy the sweet songs of praise and thanksgiving must come. If the Spirit commands us to sing when we are merry, how much more then should we be merry without mixture when we shall sing joyful hallelujahs and hosannas to Him who dwells in the highest Heaven. Our hearts shall be so full that we cannot choose but sing, and that most melodiously. There shall be no discord in this music, no end of this song. O what a blessed change for the saints! They do nothing but weep below, and they shall do nothing but sing in Heaven. We sow in tears, we reap in joy. There was some comfort in those tears, but there is no danger of complaint in this heavenly mirth. If we find we cannot sing, "peace on earth," with the angels here: yet we shall sing with them in Heaven, "Glory to God on high." We shall join our voices to theirs, we shall have that celestial comfort which none can have a part in without being happy.

RULE FIVE

There must now be a consideration of the subject. In what does it consist? Where is it employed?

"And indeed the very place where this glory is exhibited promises happiness. For it is no other than the Paradise of God. Here below we dwell, or rather we wander, in a continued wilderness. There we shall be resting in the true Eden, "I have come to My garden, My sister, My spouse." Kings do not usually dwell in houses of clay. They live in royal courts fit for their estate. How much more shall the King of Heaven do so, who has prepared such fine mansions on earth for men. Shall He not make for Himself a habitation suitable to His majesty? Even earthly kings have dwelt in cedar and ivory, but the great city, the Holy Jerusalem, the Palace of the Highest, has walls of jasper, its building of gold, its foundation of precious stones, its gates of pearls. What glorious things are spoken of you, O City of God! We see but the pavement, how good it is. O Saviour, when Thou wert in Thy humbled estate, in the form of a servant, then the believing centurion thought himself unworthy for Thee to come under his roof. How then shall I think myself worthy to come under Thy roof now that Thou art shining and glorious? O, if this clay of mine may come to such an honor above, then let it be trampled upon and despised on earth!"

RULE SIX

Consider the appendances and qualities of the subject.

But even if the place were less nobel, less majestic, yet the companionship which it affords is enough to make the soul blessed. For it is not the place which adorns the guest, but it is the guest which adorns the place. How loath we are to leave this earth, and that only because of the society of some few friends in whom we delight. Yet even these are subject every day to mutual aversions. What pleasure shall there be, then, in the company of the saints above? For there shall be nothing in them which is not amiable, nothing in us which will cool the fervor of our love. There, O my soul, you shall be glorified, and there you shall meet with your Parents and friends, also glorious. There you shall see and converse with those ancient and worthy saints of the former ages, the blessed patriarchs, the beloved prophets, the martyrs and confessors who have been crowned, the holy Apostles, the primitive fathers, those of our present age. And each shall be shining according to the measure of his blessed labors. there you shall live familiarly in the sight of the angels, the very ones who are now doing you good, though you do not see them.

"And there you shall see Him who is the Head of all your happiness. Your eyes shall see Him, the One your heart now longs for, the Saviour, who only can give you hope now. How dimly, how distantly do you now behold Him! How imperfectly do you now enjoy Him! ("I sought Him whom my soul loves; I sought Him, but found Him not"—Song of Solomon 3:1) Now, because of your sins, His back seems to be toward you, and so you can hardly discern Him. Other times you turn your back on Him through negligence, etc., when you might obscurely see Him and do not. Now you shall see Him in glory, your eyes shall be fixed, they shall never be moved.

Yet this glory would not make us so happy if it were not perpetual. To be happy is not such a sweet state if we must consider the misery of possible future unhappiness. Lest anything should be lacking in heavenly happiness, behold, this happiness has no end. It does not fear an intermission, it is eternal, as eternal as the One who had no beginning. O blessedness truly infinite! Our earthly joys scarcely ever begin, but when they do begin their end is next to the beginning. In but an hour we oftentimes are both joyful and miserable. But there, and there only, shall there be nothing but joy for an eternity. If the prophet thought that one day in the earthly house of the Lord was better than a thousand elsewhere, how shall it compare to thousands of millions, endless years of God's heavenly Temple? Yea, millions of years are not as much as a minute to eternity, and that other house was not so much as a cottage compared to the heavenly abode.

RULE SEVEN

Consider that which is different, or contrary, to it.

Let us leave for a while the consideration of the thing itself and meditate upon that which is different from it, or contrary to it.

"What are you doing here, O my soul? What are you doing here, groveling upon earth? The best things here are vanity, the rest are no better than vexation. Look around you, see whether your eyes meet with anything but sin or misery. Those few, short pleasures you see always end in sorrow, and in the meantime they are mixed with many grievances.

"And what do you hear here? Some cry out of sick bodies, the parts of which are subject to various diseases. One lays his hand on his consuming lungs and complains of short wind. Another cries of his rising spleen, a third of his painful head. Another roars because of the torment from his heart or bladder, another for the racking pain of gouty joints. One is distimpered with dropsie, another with colic, a third with ague, a fourth with epilepsy, and another is bedridden with paralysis. There are few bodies that do not complain of some illness. And, that you may look no farther, it would be a wonder if you yourself do not feel one of these evils within.

"There you hear another lament his loss; his estate is impaired by stealth, shipwreck, oppression, etc. Another cries his child is unruly, or has miscarried; another's wife is dead, or disloyal. Another is torment with passions. Each one is miserable in some way.

"Even more irksome is that your ear is beaten with cursings and blasphemies; and the other ear is beaten with scornful, wanton, or hateful speeches. Your eyes see nothing but pride, filthiness of the flesh, profaneness, excess. And whatever else might be found to vex a righteous soul, you find enough corruption within your own self to make you weary and your life loathsome. You do not need to bring causes of complaint from others, for your own corruptions yield too much for you at home. For you are ever sinning, ever presuming—sinning even when you have repented; yea, even when you repent, sinning.

"Come, my soul, solace yourself here below, allow yourself to be drunk with these contentments. See if you can find any of these things above. See if you can find any distemper, any loss, any sin, any complaint--either from yourself, or from others.

"If all this cannot commend to you the state of heavenly glory, cast your eyes down into that deep and bottomless pit, full of horror, full of torment, where there is nothing but tears and shrieks and gnashing of teeth, nothing but fiends and tortures. Look where there is darkness that can be felt, yet where there is perpetual fire; where the condemned are ever burning, but never consumed; where they are ever dying, but are never dead. Look where there is constant complaining, never any mercy; where the glutton begs for a drop of water, yet, alas, whole rivers of water would not quench those rivers of brimstone which feed this flame! Look where endless pain has no intermission, where after millions of years there will still be no possibility of comfort.

"O if the rod with which Thou dost chastise Thy children in this life is so galling, O Lord, they who have been brought down to the brink of despair, when in the bitterness of their souls they have begged for death to release them, then what shall I think of the plagues which Thou hast denounced upon those, of whom Thou hast said, "Vengeance is Mine, I will repay."

"O my soul, it is some kind of happiness to know that you shall not be so miserable as the reprobate. But the happiness that you shall have is more to be esteemed than you are now capable of.

RULE EIGHT

Consider comparisons and similitudes of the subject. To meditate on those things that most nearly resemble it, to seek the most suitable similitudes, gives great light to the understanding and adds force to the affections.

"As much as you can, O my soul, wonder at this great glory. And compare it with this earth, which you are now treading upon. One day when you are above, when you look down on the sons of men creeping like so many ants on this mole-hill of earth, you shall think, Alas, how basely I once lived. Was yonder silly dungeon the place I so dearly loved, the place I hated to leave? Think it now, think of earth, what it is worthy. If you can't give Heaven its due, you can at least give earth its due.

"How heartless and irksome are the best earthly pleasures. How cheap are you, O sumptuous buildings of kings, in comparison with this perfect tabernacle not made with hands (Hebrews 9:11). We may see the face of Heaven from the earth, but who can see the least of the glory of Heaven from any part of the earth? The three disciples saw but a glimpse of this glory shining from the face of their Saviour, yet being ravished with the sight they cried out, Master, it is good for us to be here. And they thought of building three tabernacles for Christ, Moses and Elijah, thinking they would be content to lie there without any shelter for themselves, if only they could be allowed to enjoy the sight before them. But, O my soul, how could earthly tabernacles have fitted those heavenly bodies? They knew what they saw, those disciples, but they did not know what they were saying. These three disciples were not transfigured themselves, yet how deeply they were affected by the glory of others. How happy we shall be when we shall be changed into the glorious image of Christ! Then we shall not have tabernacles of our own making, but those that were prepared for us by God.

"Moses saw God but a little while. Yet his face shone. How shall we shine when we behold His face forever!

"There is great honor in sovereignty. And there is great pleasure in feasting. This life above is both a feast and a kingdom. It is a kingdom, for it is written, "He that overcomes shall rule the nations, and he shall sit with Me in my throne." O blessed promotion. O large dominion, O royal seat! Solomon's throne of ivory was not worthy to be a footstool to this. It is a feast, for it is written, "Blessed are they that are called to the marriage of the Lamb." Feasts have more provisions than are necessary.

But marriage feasts have even more abundance. What, then, shall not the marriage feast of the Son of God to His blessed spouse (the Church) as far exceed in all heavenly munificence and variety as the persons are of the greater state and majesty? There shall be new wine, pure manna, all kinds of spiritual dainties! And with the continual cheer, there shall be a warm and amiable welcome, as the Bridegroom cheers us up. O yes, my soul, you shall be there. And you shall not be a guest, however unworthy you may be, but you shall be the bride herself, whom He has everlastingly espoused to Himself in truth and righteousness.

"The contract is made here below, the marriage is consummated above, solemnized with a perpetual feast. So you may even now safely say, "My wellbeloved is mine, and I am His. Then hearken, O my soul, incline your ear, forget your own people, your father's house, that which you call home in this world: the King shall take pleasure in your beauty, for He is the Lord. Then worship Him.

RULE NINE

Consider the titles and names of the thing considered, for these yield great increase to our meditation. Names and titles are commonly imposed so that they secretly comprehend the nature of the thing which they represent, and as such they are worth our thoughts.

"Why do I need to seek these resemblances when the very name of life implies sweetness to men on earth—even to those who confess they live with some discontentment? Surely the light is a very pleasing thing, it is good to the eyes to see the sun. Life seems good until you put temporal before it. This adding of temporary subtracts something, it greatly abates the pleasure of life. For those who rejoice to think of life also grieve to think it is but temporary. It is so vexing to us because we would like to think that that which is delightful will have continuance.

"But now, then, add to life eternity: Is not life not as much more sweet as it is much more lasting? And if it lasts infinitely, does it not give an infinite contentment?

"O what a dying and false life we enjoy here! It is scarcely more than a shadow, a counterfeit of that other life. What is more esteemed here than glory? It is so precious to men of spirit that it makes them reckless with their blood, proud of their wounds, careless of their welfare. Yet, alas, how fading is this glory which is bought with such dangers, and even with death! The trophies and monuments hardly survive the one who dies for them. But, O my soul, it is true glory to triumph in Heaven, for there neither envy nor forgetfulness is known.

"What is more dear to us than our country? Our worthy and faithful patriots have loved it more than their parents, more than their children, than their very lives. They have been not only happy to live in it, but happy to die for it. The banished man pines for it, the traveler digests all the tediousness of his way, all the sorrows of an ill journey, only because of the hope of home. Where is our country? Is it not above? From there you came, O my soul, and there you shall return after this short, weary pilgrimage. O miserable men! If we count ourselves to be at home in this land, the land of our pilgrimage, how much more ought we to long for our heavenly Home? Do you not see men so in love with their native soil that even when it is deformed with the desolations of war, turned into rude heaps, even when it is flaming with the fire of civil war, they still covet to live in it. They prefer it to all other places, however more peaceful and pleasant they may be. And shall you, O heaven-bound pilgrim, content yourself with only a faint wish for dissolution when you see nothing but trouble here and nothing but peace and blessedness at Home? O what affection could be worthy of such a Home as we have above?

RULE TEN

Consider the testimonies of Scripture which are suitable to your theme. Why consider Scriptures? Because in these matters of God, there is nothing but Divine authority which can command us. Only this will settle our conscience. The witness of holy men may serve for colors, but the ground must be only from God.

"The Holy Spirit of God says, He who cannot deceive you, that all tears shall be wiped from our eyes, there shall be no more death, no sorrow, no crying, neither shall there be any more pain.' Yea, there shall not only be an end of sorrows, but there shall be an abundant recompence for the sorrows of our life here. He who was rapt up to the third heaven and there saw what cannot be spoken yet speaks this much of what he saw, 'I judge that the afflictions of this present time are not worthy of the glory which shall be revealed to us.' It was shown to him the things which shall hereafter be shown to us. And he judged that if all the world full of miseries were laid in one balance, and the least glory of Heaven in another, those would be incomparably light. Yea, as one divine father said, one days felicity above is worth a thousand years of torment below. What then can be matched with the eternity of such joys? O how great is Thy goodness, Lord, which Thou hast laid up for those who fear thee!

THE SECOND PART OF MEDITATION: IN OUR AFFECTIONS

The most difficult and knotty part of meditation (cogitation) being finished, there remains that which is more lively and more easing to a good heart, to be wrought together by the affections. For if our meditations do not reach to the affections, they are vain and to no purpose. This that follows, then, is the very soul of meditation, and all that is past serves only as an instrument. A man is a man because of his understanding part. A man is a Christian by his will and affections. Since, then, all our former labor of the brain is only to move the heart, we must try to find some feeling touch and sweet relish in that which the mind has chewed upon. This is the fruit which, by God's blessing, will voluntarily follow a serious meditation. David cries, "O taste and see how sweet the Lord is." In meditation we aim both to see and to taste, but we see before we taste. Sight is of the understanding. Taste is of the affection. Nor can we see without tasting. We cannot know aright unless we are moved in our affections. Therefore, let the heart first conceive and feel in itself the sweetness or bitterness of the matter meditated. This is never done without some passion, or expressed without some heart exclamation.

"O blessed estate of the saints! O glory not to be expressed, no not even by those who are glorified! O incomprehensible salvation! What satisfaction can this earth have for you? Who can love the world and still believe that he is eternally saved and bound for Heaven? Who can think of such salvation and not be ravished with wonder and desire? Who can hope for it and not rejoice? Who can know this salvation and not be swallowed up with admiration for the mercy of God that bestows it? O what blessedness, that it is worth the blood of Christ! Truly it is worthy of the continual songs of both saints and angels. O how can I magnify Thee! How should I long for Thee! How I should hate the world for Thy sake!

MEDITATION AND AFFECTIONS: OUR COMPLAINT

After this seeing and tasting, there should follow a complaint. The heart should bewail its poverty, its dullness, its imperfection. It should chide and abase itself because of its deficiency and indisposition. And in this humiliation truly goes before glory. For the more we are cast down in our conceit, the higher God shall lift us up at the end of this exercise in spiritual rejoicing.

"But, alas, where is my love? Where is my longing? Where are you, O my soul? What heaviness has overtaken you? How has the world bewitched and possessed you that you have become so careless of your home, so senseless of spiritual delights, so fond of these vanities? Do you doubt that there is a Heaven? Do you doubt that you have a God, a Saviour there? O far be it from you, this abominable atheism! Let the least thought of this desperate impiety be far from you. Woe unto you if you do not believe! O soul of little faith, do you believe there is happiness, happiness for you? And do you not desire it, do you not delight in it? Alas, how weak and unbelieving is your belief! How cold and faint are your desires!

Tell me, what kind of comfort and satisfaction have you met with here on earth that you are willing to withdraw from these heavenly joys? What pleasure in this world ever gave you any contentment? Or what do you dislike about that which is above?

O my soul, it is the miserable drowsiness of the flesh, only a false security which makes you feel like this. The world, O the world has made you drunk, you are undone with carelessness. Ah, if your delight is so cold, what difference is there between you and an ignorant heathen who doubts of another life? Yea, what is the difference between you and the epicure who denies it? Are you a Christian, or are you not? If you are what you profess to be, then away with this dull and senseless worldliness, away with this earthly cheerlessness. Shake off this profane and godless security which has long weighed you down, which has kept your joys from mounting up on heavenly wings. Look up to your God, to your crown, and say with confidence, 'O Lord, I have waited for Thy salvation.'

MEDITATION AND AFFECTIONS: A HEARTY WISH

After this complaint, the soul must bring forth a hearty and passionate wish, a wish which comes from the two former steps of meditation. For if a man finds that which is sweet and comfortable, and if he complains because he still wants something, then he cannot but make a hearty wish to enjoy that which he lacks.

"O Lord, I wish that I could long for Thy salvation! O that I could mind the things that are above. O that my eyes, like the eyes of the first martyr, could by the light of faith see but a glimpse of Heaven! O that my heart could be rapt up there in desire! O then I would trample upon these poor vanities of the earth! How willingly I then would endure all sorrows, all torments. How scornfully I would then pass by all pleasures. What travail I would then be in until my dissolution! O when shall that blessed Day come, the Day when all this wretched worldliness shall be removed, when I shall solace myself in my God? Behold! As the hart pants for the rivers of waters, so my soul pants after Thee, O my God! "My soul thirsts for God, even for the living God, O when shall I come and appear in the presence of God?'"

MEDITATION AND AFFECTIONS: A HUMBLE CONFESSION

After this wishing, by just order of nature, humble confession should follow. For when we have bemoaned our want and wished for supply, not finding this hope in ourselves we must acknowledge it to Him. For it is of Him that we may seek and find. And in this matter we must observe how the mind is by turns depressed and lifted up. It is lifted up with our taste of joy, then it is cast down by our complaint; it is lifted up with our wishes, it is cast down by our confession. And it is best to hold it in this order, for it will make us more feeling of the comfort which follows in the end. This confession must take away everything from ourselves, it must ascribe all to God.

"This I desire, O Lord, to be rightly affected towards Thee and Thy glory. But, alas! How weak I am! How heartless I am! Thou dost know that I can neither come to Thee nor desire to come. It is my nature that holds me away from Thee, this treacherous nature favors itself, loves the world, hates to think of being dissolved. It would rather dwell in this dungeon with continual sorrow and complaint than to endure a parting, even though it be to liberty and joy. Alas, Lord, it is my misery that I love my pain. How long shall these vanities befuddle me? Thou alone canst turn my eyes away from these follies, Thou canst keep my heart from loving them. Thou art the one, and Thou only, who can fix my soul upon Heaven and Thee, even as Thou art the one who shall one day receive my soul into that Heaven.

MEDITATION AND AFFECTIONS: AN EARNEST PETITION

After confession, petition naturally follows. There will be an earnest request that God will perform that which we are not able to perform.

"O carry up my soul, Thou who hast created and redeemed it, carry it up to Thy glory. O do not let me be always so dull and brutish. Do not let these scales of earthly affection always dim and blind my eyes. O Thou who dost lay clay upon the blind man's eyes, please take away this clay from my eyes, for they are so bedaubed that they cannot see Heaven. Illuminate them from above, O Lord, in Thy light let me see light. O Thou who hast prepared a place for my soul, please prepare my soul for that place. Prepare it with holiness, prepare it with desire; even when it remains on earth let it dwell in Heaven with Thee, beholding forever the beauty of Thy face, the glory of Thy saints.

MEDITATION AND AFFECTIONS: THE PETITION ENFORCED

After petition, enforcement of our request should follow, both by argument and by importunate supplication. But in this we must avoid flattering words, knowing that God will not be mocked by any fashionable form of petition, knowing that He requires only a holy and feeling entreaty.

"O heavenly Father, how graciously Thou hast proclaimed to the world that he who lacks wisdom should ask it of Thee, that Thou wilt never deny him nor upbraid him. O Lord, I lack heavenly wisdom, I cannot conceive aright of Heaven. I lack it and I ask it of Thee. O give it to me instantly, give it to me abundantly according to Thy promise. Thou dost see that it is not a strange favor that I ask of Thee, for it is nothing else than that which Thou hast so richly bestowed upon all Thy valiant martyrs, confessors, servants, from the beginning. For these could never have so cheerfully embraced death and torment if they had not seen their crown of glory through the midst of their flames and pain. The poor thief on the cross had no sooner craved Thy remembrance when Thou didst come into Thy Kingdom than Thou didst promise to take him with Thee into Heaven. Thy presence then was better to him than remembrance. Behold, Thou art now in Thy Kingdom, I am on earth. Remember Thy unworthy servant, let my soul in thought, in affection, in all it does, be today and forever with Thee in Paradise. I see men walking in vain shadows, I see them disquiet themselves in vain. The pleasures he enjoys are pitiful, and all the while he forgets Thee. I am just as vain, make me more wise. O let me see Heaven and I know I shall never envy or follow them. My times are in Thy hands, I am no better than my fathers, I am a stranger on earth. And as I speak this of them, so the next generation shall speak of me as one that was. My life is but a bubble, a smoke, a shadow, a thought. I know there is nothing that abides in this thoroughfare. O do not allow me to be so mad as to forget the end while I pass on the way. It is that other life that I must trust to. With Thee it is that I shall continue. O let me not be so foolish as to settle myself on what I must leave, neglecting eternity. I have seen enough of this earth, yet I love it too much. O let me see Heaven for a while, and let me love it so much more than the earth, even as much as there are things there more worthy to be loved. O my God, look down on Thy wretched pilgrim. Teach me to look up unto Thee, to see Thy goodness in the land of the living. O Thou who hast bought Heaven for me, guide me there. For the price that it cost Thee, for Thy mercies' sake, in spite of all temptations, enlighten my soul, direct it, crown it.

MEDITATION AND AFFECTIONS: A CHEERFUL CONFIDENCE

After this enforcement, confidence should follow. After many doubts and unquiet bickerings, the soul gathers up her forces and cheerfully rouses itself. Like one of David's mighty men, it breaks through a whole army of doubts, it brings forth comfort from the Well of Life, knowing that there shall be a sure reward from God for sincere meditation.

"Be bold, O my soul, do not merely crave. Challenge the favor of God, as if He owed it to you. He owes it to you because He has promised it, and by His mercy He has made this gift to be His debt. "Faithful is He that has promised, who also will do it.' Has He not given you not only His hand in the sweet hopes of the Gospel, but also His seal in the sacraments? Yea, besides His promise, His hand, His seal, has He not given you a sure earnest of your salvation in true graces? And more, besides this earnest, has He not give you possession. For He who is the Truth and the Life says, "He that believes has everlasting life and has passed from death unto life.' O, then, can you not be content to cast yourself upon this blessed issue? If God is merciful, I am glorious, for I have Him already. God is faithful, and I do believe: who shall separate me from the love of Christ? from my glory with Christ? Who shall pull me out of my Heaven? O my soul, return to your rest, make use of the Heaven in which you are and be happy with it.

THE CONCLUSION OF MEDITATION: WITH THANKSGIVING

So we have found that our meditation, like the wind, gathers strength as it goes. As natural bodies, the nearer they come to their places, the more quickly they move, so does the soul move with more celerity in this course of meditation, to the unspeakable benefit of itself.

In conclusion, we must not cease too suddenly, but we must leave off by little and little. The mind must not be allowed to fall headlong from this height, it must also descend by degrees.

The first concluding step, then, should be a hearty rejoicing and thanksgiving. When a man is miserable, it is natural for him to complain and crave remedy. So a good heart cannot find itself happy unless it is thankful. And this thankfulness which it feels and expresses makes it even happier, affects it even more.

"What, then, shall I do for Thee because of this mercy, O Saviour of men? What should I render to my Lord for all His benefits? Alas! What can I give Thee which is not Thine own already? Thou dost give me to drink of this cup of salvation, therefore I will take the cup of salvation and call upon the name of the Lord. 'Praise the Lord, O my soul, and all that is within me praise His holy name.' And, O soul of mine, since you begin your heaven here, begin here also that joyful song of thanksgiving which you shall sing there the more sweetly and without end.

THE CONCLUSION OF MEDITATION: COMMITTING OUR WAYS

After this thanksgiving, a faithful recommendation of ourselves to God shall follow. In this the soul cheerfully gives itself up and reposes itself wholly upon its Maker and Redeemer. It commits itself to Him in all its ways, submitting itself to Him in all His ways, desiring in all things to glorify Him, to walk worthy of its high and glorious calling.

THE CONCLUSION OF MEDITATION: SING A PSALM

Both the latter steps may be done (as I have experienced) with much life and comfort by lifting up our heart and voice to God in singing some verse or two of David's Psalms (one that answers to our disposition and the matter of our meditation). In this way the heart closes up with much sweetness and contentment.

Having heartily observed this course of meditation, tell me if you do not find that your soul (which groveled on the earth at the beginning of the exercise) does not now in the end soar aloft into Heaven? If it was aloof before, does it not now find itself near to God? Yea, is it not with Him and in Him?

AN EPILOGUE

So I have endeavored, according to my slender ability, to pre-scribe a method of meditation. I do so without any strict terms of necessity, as if whoever does not go my way shall err. But often different paths lead to the same end, and every man abounds in his own sense. If experience and custom have made another form fam-iliar to anyone, I do not forbid it. As that learned father said of his translation, 'Let him use his own, not condemn mine.' If any-one chooses to do so, let him practice my method, until he meets a better master. If another course may be better, I am sure this is good. Some eccentric men, while they have doubts as to which fashionable suit they shall wear, put on nothing. Such must not be allowed in regard to meditation. We Christians should not neglect the matter of this worthy business while we nicely stand upon the form of it.

Give me permission to complain with just sorrow and shame that there is no Christian duty whose neglect and omission is more shameful and prejudicial to the souls of professors than this one of meditation. This is the very reason God has given us souls! We misspend them if we do not use them in this way. How lamentable it is that we employ them as if our faculty of meditation served for nothing but our earthly provision. As if our reasonable and Christian minds were appointed for the slavery and drudgery of this body, only to be the caterers and cooks for our appetites.

The world fills us, yea, it cloys us. We find ourselves thinking, "What do I have? How can I get more? What must I do? What shall I leave for my children? How can I prevent my adversary from do-ing me harm? How can I return it? What answers shall I make to such and such allegations? What entertainment shall I give to my friends? What courses shall I take in such and such suits? In what pastimes shall I spend today? What advantage shall I reap by this practice? What loss? What was said, what was answered, what was done, what followed that, etc."

Are these the beautiful thoughts that are fit for spiritual minds? Even if there were no other world, how could we spend our cares this way? It is the neglect of meditation which causes the common Laodicean temper of men. It causes the dead coldness which has stricken the hearts of many, leaving them nothing but the bodies of men and the visors of Christians. I say, it may be ascribed to this: THEY HAVE NOT MEDITATED!

It is no more impossible to live without a heart than to be devout without meditation. O that God might make my words to be like goads in the sides of every reader, to enliven him, to startle him out of his dull and lazy security, to begin the cheerful practice of divine meditation. Let him curse me upon his deathbed if, looking back from there to his former times, he does not acknowledge that these hours of meditation are not the most happy hours in his whole life. Yea, he will then wish that he had worn out more days in such profitable and heavenly a work.

JOSEPH HALL
Bishop of Norwich

A MEDITATION OF DEATH
(according to the former rules)

THE ENTRANCE INTO THE SUBJECT OF DEATH
"And now, my soul, that you have thought of the end, what could
be more suitable than to think of the way? And though the fore-
part of the way to Heaven is a good life, the latter and more immediate is death. Shall I call death the way? Or shall I call it the
gate to life? Of this I am sure, that it is only through death that
we pass into that blessedness of which we have been thinking (and
we have found that it cannot be enough thought of).

THE DESCRIPTION
What then is this death? Is it not but the taking down of these
sticks of which this earthly tent is composed? Is it not but the
separations of two great and old friends until they meet again? Is
it not the delivery of a long-time prisoner from jail? Is this not
the journey into that other world for which we and this thoroughfare were made? Is it not our payment of our first debt to nature,
the sleep of the body, and the awaking of the soul?

THE DIVISION INTO PARTS
But lest you should seem to flatter death, whose name and face
has ever seemed terrible to others, remember that there are more
deaths than one. If the first death is not as fearful as it is made
out to be (its horror lying more in the imagination of the beholder
than in its own aspect,)surely the second death is not made nearly
as fearful as it truly is. No living eye can behold the terrors of
the second death. It is impossible to see them, as impossible as
to feel them and still live. Nothing but a name is common to both
these deaths. The first has men, accidents, diseases as its exe-
cutioners, but the second has devils. The power of the first death
is in the grave. The power of the second death is in hell. The worse
of the first death is senselessness. The easiest of the second
death is a perpetual sense of all the pain that can make a man ex-
quisitely miserable.

THE CAUSES
"You shall have no business with the second death, O my soul,
for your first resurrection has made you safe. Thank Him who has
redeemed you, thank Him for your safety. And how can I thank
Thee enough, O my Saviour, Thou who hast so mercifully bought off
my torment with Thy own; Thou who hast drunk that bitter potion
of the Father's wrath which would have been our death to taste.
Yea, such is Thy mercy, O Redeemer of men, that Thou hast not
only subdued the second death, but Thou hast reconciled the first

so that Thy children shall not taste of the second. Yea, they find the first death so sweetened by Thee that they do not complain of its bitterness. Thou were not the one who made death, O God, but our hands are guilty of this evil. Thou didst see all Thy work, that it was good. We brought forth sin and sin brought forth death. To the discharge of Thy justice and mercy, we acknowledge this miserable conception—and it is no wonder that the child is ugly, having such parents. If being and good are of an equal extent (and they are) then the dissolution of our being must in itself be evil. How full of darkness and horror then is the privation of this vital light, and more so since Thy wisdom intended it to be the revenge of sin (and sin is no less than the violation of an infinite justice). It was Thy just pleasure to plague us with this brood of our own begetting: now, behold, that death which was not in the world until then is now in everything. One great conqueror finds it in a slate, another in a fly; one finds it in the kernel of a grape, another in the prick of a thorn. One finds death in the taste of herbs, another in the smell of a flower; one in a bit of meat, another in a mouthful of air. One finds it in the very sight of a danger, another in the imagination of what might have happened. Nothing in all our life is too little to hide death under it. No cords, or knives, or swords, or anything else are needed. We have made as many ways to death as there are helps to living.

But if we were the authors of our death, it was Thou that didst alter it. Our disobedience made it, and Thy mercy removed the evil from it. Thou couldst have taken away the very being of death from Thy children, but it pleased Thee only to take away the sting of it. It is more glory to Thee that Thou hast removed enmity from this Esau, so that now he comes to meet us with kisses instead of frowns. And if we receive a blow from this rough hand, yet that very stripe is healing. O how much more powerful is Thy death than our sin! O my Saviour, Thou hast perfumed and softened the bed of my grave, by Thy dying. How can it grieve me to tread in Thy steps to glory?

THE EFFECTS

Our sin made death our last enemy; Thy goodness has made it the first friend that we meet in our passage to another world. For as she who receives us from the knees of our mother in our first entrance to the light of this world, so death is the first one that receives us in our passage to that other life. It is death that presents our naked souls to the hands of the angels who are to carry it up to glory. Should we not then count death as friendly, meritorious? What if this guide leads my carcase through corruption and rottenness? Still, my soul knows in the very instant of its separation that it is happy. What if my friends mourn around my bed and coffin? Yet my soul sees the smiling face, the loving embrace of Him who was dead, but now is alive. What do I care if I must shut these earthen eyes, when death opens the eye of my soul and I can see even as I am seen? If I live above with the God of spirits, what do I care if my name is forgotten by men?

THE SUBJECT

If death still seems to be an enemy, yet is it the worst part of me that he has anything to do with. The best of me is above its reach. The worst horror of death is the grave. And, setting aside unfaithfulness, what is so miserable about that? That part which is corrupted (the body) does not feel it. That which is free from corruption feels an abundant recompence and foresees a joyful reparation. What is there here but a just restitution? We carry Heaven and earth wrapped up in our bosoms: each part returns homeward. And if the exceeding glory of Heaven cannot countervail the dolesomeness of the grave, what business do I have in believing? But if the beauty of that celestial sanctuary more than equalizes the horror of the bottomless pit, how can I shrink at earth like myself when I know my glory?

And if examples cannot move you a whit, look behind you, O my soul, and see which of the patriarchs, kings, prophets and apostles have failed to tread these red steps. Where are those millions of generations which have peopled the earth before now? How many tolling bells have you heard for your known friends? How many sick-beds have you visited? How many eyes have you seen closed? How many vain men have you seen going into the field to seek death, only in the hope of finding an honor as foolish as themselves? How many of the creatures have you deprived of life for your very own pleasure? And can you hope that God will make a bypass of death for you alone, so that you may pass into the next world by some other gate besides death?

THE ADJUNCT

What, then, do you fear, O my soul? There are but two stages of death; the bed and the grave. The grave has senselessness, but it also has rest. The deathbed has pain, yet it also has speediness. When it lights upon a faithful heart, it meets with many strong antidotes of comfort. The evil that is ever in motion is not fearful. That which both time and eternity finds standing where it was is worthy of terror. Well may those who find more distress within than without tremble at death. If their conscience is more sickly and nearer to death than their bodies, they should tremble. It was Thy Father's wrath which so terrified Thy soul, O my Saviour, so that Thy body didst break into a bloody sweat. The mention and thought of Thy death ended in a Psalm, but this began in an agony. It was then that Thou didst sweat out my fears. The power of that agony comforts all Thy children more than the angels could comfort Thee. That very voice deserved an eternal separation from the horror of death, when Thou didst cry, "My God, My God, why hast Thou forsaken Me?" Thou wouldst not have complained about being left if Thou wouldst have any of Thine left destitute of comfort in their parting. I do not know whom I can fear, but I know whom I have believed. How can I be discouraged at the sight of death when I see so clearly the advantage of it?

THAT WHICH IS CONTRARY

How is this a discomfort, to leave a frail body and be joined to a glorious Head? To forsake vain pleasures, false honors, worthless hopes, unsatisfying wealth, stormy contentments, sinful men, perilous temptations, a sea of troubles, a galley of servitude, an evil world, and a consuming life in order to receive freedom, rest, happiness and eternal life is no discomfort. And if you were sentenced to live a thousand years in this body, O my soul, would you not be weary of these infirmities, of this being, even of complaining? Before the first hundred years, I would be a child; before the second hundred, a beast. Before the third hundred years, I would be no more than a stone—so far from finding pleasure in continuing, I would not have sense enough left to feel miserable. And once I am gone, what difference is there between the oldest of the first patriarchs and me?

Even if this body had no weakness to make my life tedious, yet what a torment it is to know that while I live I must sin? Alas, my soul, every one of your known sins is not a disease but a death. What an enemy you are to yourself if you cannot be content that one bodily death should excuse you from many spiritual deaths. Should you not be content to cast off your body so that you may be stripped of your rags, yea, the fetters of your sin, so that you may be clothed with the robes of glory? Yet these terms are too hard, for the body shall not be cast off, rather it shall be changed to be no less happy a partner of the glorified soul. This very skin of mine, tawny and wrinkled, shall one day shine. This earth shall be Heaven, this dust shall be glorious. These eyes which are now so weary of witnessing your sins and miseries shall then never be weary of seeing the beauty of Thy Saviour. These ears, now tormented with the impious tongues of men, shall first hear the voice of the Son of God, then the voices of the saints and angels in their songs of Hallelujah! And the tongue that now complains of miseries and tears shall then bear a part in that divine harmony.

THE COMPARISONS

In the meantime you but sleep in this bed of earth. He who has tried the worst of death has called it no worse than sleep. Very heathens have termed them cousins. Have you ever been reluctant to lie down to rest when the day has wearied you? Behold, in this sleep of death, there is more quietness, more pleasures in visions, more certainty of waking, more cheerfulness in rising. When, then, are you going to be content to lay off your rags, to rest yourself quietly? Why are you like a child unwilling to go to bed? Is there a bird which, when the cage was opened, would rather sit and sing inside her bars than to fly forth to her freedom? Have you ever seen a prisoner in love with his bars and chains? When the angel of God struck Peter on the side and loosed his chains and told him to arise and flee, did Peter say, What! so soon? Let me sleep a little? Have you ever seen a mariner who has saluted the sea with songs and the haven with tears? What shall I say to your diffidence, O my soul, that you are unwilling to think of rest after your toil, of freedom after your imprisonment, of the haven after an unquiet and tempestuous passage? How many are there who seek death and cannot find it, merely because of the irksomeness of life! Has it found you, offering you better conditions (not of immunity from evils, but of possession of more good,) and would you now flee from happiness, try to be rid of it?

THE NAMES

What? Is it a name that troubles you? What if men would call sleep death, would you then be afraid to close your eyes? If God sent the first sleep upon man while He made him a helper, what hurt is it if He sends this last sound sleep upon me while He prepares my soul for a glorious spouse to Himself? That which we call death is but a parting. The soul will return laden with the riches of Heaven and will bring his old partner, the body, into the participation of this glorious wealth. Go, my soul, to this sure and gainful business, leave the other half in a harbor so safe (though not so blessed).

THE TESTIMONIES OF SCRIPTURE

Were you so unwilling to join this body of mine at the first, at the command of your Creator, O soul? Why then are you so loath to part with that which you have found to be so troublesome? Do you not hear Solomon say, "the day of death is better than the day of your birth." Do you not believe him? Are you in love with the worst and displeased with the best? If anyone could have found a life worthy to be preferred to death, such a great king must have been the one. Yet now, in his very throne, he commends his coffin. Yea, what will you say to those heathen who have mourned at the birth and feasted at the death of their children? They knew the miseries of living as well as you, but the happiness of dying they could not know. If they rejoiced because death was a cessation of misery, how ought you to cheer yourself in an expectation, yea an assurance of being happy! He who is Lord of life, who has experienced what it is to die, has proclaimed those who die in the Lord to be blessed. Those who live in Him are blessed, I know, but they are not able to rest from their labors. Toil and sorrow is between them and that perfect enjoyment of blessedness which they now possess only in hope. When death has added rest, their happiness will be complete.

THE TASTE OF OUR MEDITATION

O death, how sweet is that rest with which you refresh the weary pilgrims of this vale of mortality! How pleasant your face is to those eyes that have acquainted themselves with the sight of it (yet to strangers it is grim and ghastly). How worthy you are to be welcome to those who know where you come from and where you lead to. Who that knows you can fear you? Who (that is not all nature) would rather hide himself among the baggage of this vile life than to follow you to a crown? What indifferent judge could look at this painted life (with its vain semblances of pleasures attended with sorrows on one side and uncertainty of continuance on the other) and then turn his eyes upon death (black, but comely, attended on the one hand with a momentary pain, but with eternity of glory on the other) and not say that which the prophet said out of passion, "It is better for me to die than to live."

THE COMPLAINT

But, O my soul, what ails you that you are suddenly so backward and fearful? No heart has more freely discoursed of death, in speculation, no tongue has more extolled it in absence. And now that it has come to your bedside and has drawn your curtains, you shrink inwardly; by the paleness of your face and wildness of your eyes, you betray an amazement at the presence of such a guest. That face, so familiar to your thoughts, is now unwelcome to your eyes. I am ashamed of this weak irresolution. What has Christianity done for you, if you still fear death like the heathen? Is this your imitation of the many worthy saints of God who have entertained the most violent deaths with smiles and songs? Is this the fruit of your long and frequent instruction? Did you think death would have been content with words? Did you hope it would be enough for you to talk? Where is your faith? Is Heaven worthy of no more thanks, no more joy? Shall heretics and pagans give death a better welcome than you do? Has your Maker, your Redeemer sent for you, and are you unwilling to go? Has God sent His angels to bring you, and are you loath to go? Rouse up yourself for shame, O my soul, and if you have truly believed, shake off this unchristian diffidence and dress yourself joyfully for your glory.

THE WISH

Yea, O my Lord, it is Thou who must raise up this faint and drooping heart of mine. Thou alone canst rid me of this weak and cowardly distrust. Thou dost send for my soul, and Thou canst prepare it for Thyself. Thou alone canst make Thy messenger welcome to me. O that I could but see Thy face, through death!

THE CONFESSION

But, alas, O my God, nature is strong and weak in me at the same time. I cannot wish to welcome death, as it is worthy. When I look for most courage, I find strongest temptations. I see and confess that when I am myself, Thou hast no coward such as I am. Let me alone and I shall shame Thy precious name, which I have professed. O God, were Thy martyrs thus haled to their stakes? Could they not have been loosed from their racks, yet they chose to die in those tortures? Let it be no shame unto Thy servant to take up that complaint which Thou reported of Thy better servants, "The spirit is willing, but the flesh is weak."

THE PETITION AND ENFORCEMENT

O Thou God of spirits, Thou who hast coupled soul and body together, unite them in a desire for their dissolution; weaken this flesh to receive and encourage this spirit to desire or to condemn death. And now as I grow nearer to my home, let me increase in the sense of my joys. I am Thine, save me, O Lord. It was Thou that put such courage into Thy ancient and late witnesses, so that they invited or challenged death, holding their persecutors to be their best friends for letting them loose from these fetters of flesh. I know that Thy hand is not shortened, O let Thy goodness enable me to reach them in the comfortable steadiness of my passage. Do but draw this veil a little so that I may see my glory, then I cannot be but inflamed with the desire of it. I was not the one who made this body for the earth, or this soul for my body, or Heaven for my soul, or this glory of Heaven, or this entrance into glory. It is all Thy work, O perfect what Thou hast begun, so that Thy praise and my happiness may be consummated at once.

THE ASSURANCE OR CONFIDENCE

Yea, O my soul, what need do you have to wish that the God of mercies might be tender of His own honor? Are you not a member of that body of which Thy Saviour is the Head? Can you drown when your Head is above? Was it not for you that He triumphed over death? O my Redeemer, I have already overcome in Thee, how can I miscarry in myself? O my soul, there remains nothing for you, only a crown of righteousness, which that righteous Judge shall give you at that Day. "O death, where is your sting! O grave, where is your victory?

THE THANKSGIVING

Return now unto your rest, O my soul, for the Lord has been good to you. O Lord God, the strength of my salvation, Thou hast covered my head in the day of battle. O my God and King, I will extol Thee, I will bless Thy name forever and ever. I will bless Thee daily and praise Thy name forever. Great is the Lord and most worthy to be praised; His greatness is incomprehensible. I will meditate of the beauty of Thy glorious majesty and Thy wonderful works. Hosanna, Thou that dwellest in the highest heavens.

PUBLISHER'S NOTE

SUBJECTS AND MATTER FOR MEDITATIONS

The following short meditations are furnished to those who desire to make an immediate start on the meditative trail to happiness. They are very inspiring and instructive in themselves, and they furnish matter for much further contemplation by the reader. All of them are from the pen of Bishop Hall.

SUBJECTS AND MATTER FOR MEDITATION

1. MEDITATION: Those who begin heavenly thoughts and do not prosecute them are like those who kindle a fire under green wood and leave it as soon as it begins to flame. They lose the hope of a good beginning for lack of seconding it with a suitable proceeding. When I set myself to meditate, I will not give over until I come to an issue. It has been said by some that the beginning is as much as the middle, yea, more important than all. But I say that the ending is more important than the beginning.

2. FAME AND GREATNESS: There is nothing, none but man, that respects greatness. Not God, nor death, nor judgment. God is no accepter of persons. Nature is not, for we see the sons of kings born as naked as the poorest; the poor child is born as well-favored, as beautiful, as witty, as the heir of nobles. Not disease, for it sickens all alike; not death, for all die alike; not judgment, for all fare alike after death. There is nothing, on the other hand, except man alone, which does not respect goodness. I will honor greatness in others, but for myself I will esteem a dram of goodness worth a whole world of greatness.

3. IGNORANCE: As there is a foolish wisdom, so there is a wise ignorance—in not prying into God's Ark, not inquiring into things not revealed. I would like to know all that I need to know, all that I may know, but I leave all God's secrets to Himself. It is happy for me that God makes me of His Court, not of His counsel.

4. DEPRAVITY: As there is no vacuity in nature, neither is there spiritually. Every vessel is full, if not of liquid, then of air. So it is with the heart of man. Though by nature it is empty of grace, yet it is full of hypocrisy and iniquity. As it is now filled with grace, it is emptied of its evil qualities. As in a vessel, when water goes in, air goes out. But man's heart is a narrow-mouthed vessel, it receives grace only by drops. Therefore it takes a long time for it to empty and fill. Now, as there are differences in degrees, and one heart is nearer to fullness than another, so the best vessel is not quite full while it is in the body (because there are still remainders of corruption). I will neither be content with that measure of grace which I have, nor will I be impatient with God's delay, but every day I will endeavor to have one drop added to the rest—so that my last day shall fill up my vessel to the brim.

5. HOLY LIVING: Satan would seem to be mannerly and reasonable, acting as if he would be content with half of the heart. But God challenges all or none, as He indeed has most reason to claim all, having made all. But this is nothing but a crafty trick of Satan, for he knows that if he has any part of the heart, then God

will have none. So the whole heart then falls to him. My heart (when it is whole and at its best) is but a strait and unworthy lodging for God. If it were bigger and better, I would still reserve it all for Him. Satan may look in at my doors, by a temptation, but he shall not have so much as one room set apart for him to lodge in.

6. GOSSIP: Consent hardens sin, which a little dislike would have daunted at first. As we say, There would be no thieves if there were no receivers—there would not be so many open mouths to detract and slander if there were not so many open ears to entertain them. If I cannot stop another man's mouth from speaking ill, I will either open my mouth to reprove it, or else I will stop my ears from hearing it. And I will let him see in my face that he has no room in my heart.

7. EVIL COMPANIONS: I have often wondered how fish can retain their fresh taste, yet live in salty waters. For I see that every other thing participates in the nature of the place where it abides. The waters passing through the channels of the earth vary their flavor with the veins of soil through which they slide. So, brute creatures, when they are transported from one region to another, alter their former quality and degenerate little by little. I have seen the like danger in the manners of men who converse with evil companions in corrupt places. For, besides the fact that it blemishes their reputation, causing them to be thought evil, even if they are good, it breeds in them an insensible declination to ill. And it works in them, if not an approval, yet a lesser dislike of those sins to which our ears and eyes are so continually inured. I may have a bad acquaintance, but I will never have a wicked companion.

8. GOD'S PROMISES: Some promise what they cannot do (as Satan to Christ); some what they could do, but do not intend to do (as Jacob's sons to the Shechemites); some what they meant for a time, but afterwards retract (as Laban to Jacob); some what they do also give, but unwillingly (as Herod); some what they are willing to give, but afterward repent of it (as Joshua to the Gibeonites). There is such great occasion of distrust in man, whether from his impotence, or from his faithlessness! But I see that God is not like man in this, but in whatever He promises, He proves Himself to be faithful, both in His ability and in His performance. I will therefore forever trust God on His bare word, even with hope, or besides hope, above hope, against hope. I will rely upon Him for small matters of this life also, for how shall I hope to trust Him in impossibilities if I cannot trust Him to do what is likely? How

can I depend on Him to raise my body from dust, to save my soul, if I do not trust Him for a crust of bread to preserve me?

9. LOVE OF THE WORLD: If the world would make me its servant, it could give me only what it has to give. And does the world have aught to give? It can but give a smoke of honor, a shadow of riches, a sound of pleasures, a puff of fame—which, when I have had them in their best measure, may make me worse. I could not be any better because of them. I can live not a whit longer, no merrier, no happier because of them. If the world professes to hate me, what can it do to me? It can only disgrace me in regard to my name, impoverish me in my estate, or afflict me in my body. I have been beguiled by the world and its vain appearances too long. From now on I will count myself to have been born to a better world, and I will in a holy loftiness bear myself as one too good to be in love with the best pleasures of this life, or to be daunted by the greatest miseries of it.

10. CONTENTMENT: I see there is no one so happy as to have all things. And there is no one so miserable as not to have some things. Why should I look for a better condition than others? If I have something, and that of the best things, then I will in thankfulness enjoy them. And I will lack the rest with contentment.

11. HYPOCRISY: It is the greatest madness in the world to be a hypocrite in religious profession. Men hate you because you are a Christian, even if it is only in the matter of appearance. God doubly hates you because you are only a Christian in appearance. And while you have the hatred of both God and man, you have no comfort within yourself. Yet if you will not be as good as you seem, I hold it is better to seem as evil as you are. An openly wicked man does much hurt with his notorious sins. But a hypocrite in the end shames goodness more by seeming to be good. I had rather be an openly wicked man than to be a hypocrite. But I would rather not be a man at all, than to be either of them.

12. HAPPINESS: When I look down upon my wants, upon my sins, upon miseries, I think that no one could be worse than I am. My means are so many, so full of force, almost violent. My progress is so small and insensible. My corruptions are so strong, my infirmities are so frequently noticeable and remediless. My body seems so unanswerable to my mind. But when I look up to the blessings God has enriched me with, I think that I should soon be induced to think no one could be more happy than I am. God is my friend, and He is my Father. The world is not my master, but my slave. I haven't many friends, but they are such tried and true friends that I dare trust them. My estate is not superfluous, but it is not needy—though nearer to deficiency than to abundance. If my

calling is despised by men, yet it is honorable with God. My body is not so strong as to allow a feeling of security (often checking me in an occasion of pleasure,) yet it is not so weak as to afflict me continually. My mind is not enough furnished with knowledge to allow boasting, yet it is not so naked that I need despair of obtaining knowledge. My miseries give me joy, even if they give my enemies an advantage, for my account is cast up for another world. And if you think that I have said too much good of myself, either I am this way, or at least I desire to be.

13. LOVE OF THE WORLD. Of all men, the worldling's life is most uncomfortable. For that which is his god does not always favor him. And He who should be his God never favors him.

14. COMPANIONS. I do not care for any companion unless he either teaches me something or learns something from me. Both of these give me pleasure. The one is an agent to work upon me, the other is a subject for me to work upon. I cannot tell which is more pleasure to me. For though it is an excellent thing to learn, yet I learn only to teach others.

15. HEAVEN AND EARTH. If earth (which is provided for mortality, which is possessed by the Maker's enemies) has so much pleasure in it that worldlings think it is worth being called their heaven (having such a sun to give it light, such an expanse to wall it in, such sweet fruits and flowers to adorn it, such variety of creatures to make it commodious), then what must Heaven be like? For Heaven is provided for God and His friends. How can it be of less worth than God is above His creatures, than God's friends are better than His enemies? I will not only be content to be dissolved, but I will greatly desire it.

16. WORK AND PAIN. No good thing ever comes easily. The heathen could say, "God sells knowledge for sweat and honor for jeopardy." No one ever got either wealth or learning with ease. Therefore the greatest good must be the most difficult. Then how shall I hope to get Christ if I take no pains for Him? And if in all other things the difficulty of obtaining whets the mind so much the more to seek, then why should the difficulty of seeking Christ daunt me? I will not care what I do, what I suffer, if I may but win Christ! If men can endure such cutting, such searing of the body, in order to prolong a miserable life, for just a little while, then what pain should I refuse for eternity.

17. RICHES. The world teaches me that it is madness to leave behind me those goods which I am able to carry with me. Christianity teaches me that which I charitably give while I am alive will be carried with me when I am dead. And experience teaches me that what I leave behind me will be lost. Therefore I will carry my

treasure with me by giving it away—which the worldling loses by keeping it. His corpse shall carry nothing but a winding cloth to his grave, but I shall be richer under the earth than I was above it.

18. HEAVEN AND HELL. Everyone has a heaven and a hell. Earth is the wicked man's heaven, his hell is yet to come. On the contrary, the godly have their hell on earth (where they are vexed with temptations, afflictions, by Satan and his accomplices). But their Heaven is above in endless happiness. If it go ill with me on earth, it is well that my torment is so short and easy—for I will not be so covetous as to hope for two heavens.

19. DEATH. A man on his deathbed has a double prospect, which were kept from him in his lifetime by the interposition of pleasure and miseries. The good man looks upward and with Stephen sees Heaven open and the glory of the angels who are ready to carry up his soul. The wicked man looks downward and sees three terrible spectacles: Death, Judgment, Hell—one beyond the other, all to be passed through by his soul. I do not marvel that the godly have been so cheerful in death, that those torments (the very sight of which has overcome the beholders) have seemed easy to them. I do not marvel that a wicked man is so loath to hear of death, so dejected when he feels sick, so desperate when he feels the pangs of death. It is no marvel that every Balaam should desire to die the death of the righteous. From now on I shall not envy anyone but a good man. And I will pity nothing so much as the prosperity of the wicked.

20. AFFLICTION. Not to be afflicted is a sign of weakness. For it is because of my weakness that God does not impose more afflictions upon me, for He sees that I cannot bear any more. God will never choose a weak champion. When I am stronger I will look for more afflictions. And when I can sustain more, it will be a comfort to me that God finds me strong enough to bear them—more so than it shall grieve me to be pressed heavily by affliction.

21. GODLY WARFARE. It is no wonder that the wicked have peace within themselves. For they are as secure as the temptations of their king can make them. No king ever makes war with his own subjects. The godly, however, are still enemies. Therefore they may expect to be assaulted both by stratagems and violence. Nothing shall give me more joy than my inward quietness, for a just war is a thousand times more happy than an ill-conditioned peace.

22. SIN. Goodness is so powerful that it can make things which are simply evil (namely, our sins) good to us—not good in nature, but good in the event—good when they are done, not good to be done. Sin is so powerful that it can turn the holiest ordinances of God into sin. But in this our sin goes beyond our goodness, in that sin

defiles a man or an action which is otherwise good—but all the goodness of the world cannot justify a single sin. The holy flesh in the skirt could not make the bread holy by touching it, but the unclean thing touching a holy thing could defile it. I will loath every evil for its own sake. I will do good, but I will not trust in it.

23. SUCCESS. Fools measure good actions by what happens after they are done. Wise men measure them beforehand, by judgment, upon the rules of reason and faith. Let me do well, but let God take charge of the success. If it is well accepted, it is well; but if not, my thanks is with God.

24. GROWING IN GRACE. A man who never changes is not a good man. For if he were good he would necessarily desire to be better. Grace is so sweet that whoever tastes it cannot but long for more. And if he desires it, he will try to get it. And if he so endeavors, God will crown it with success. God's family allows no dwarves (who are unthriving, stand still in growth), but it must have men who grow. Whatever may become of my body or my estate, I will ever labor to find something added to the stature of my soul.

25. PRIDE. Pride is the most dangerous of all sins. For it is most insinuative (having crept into Heaven, into Paradise), and it is most dangerous where it is. For, where all other temptations are about evil, this alone is conversant only about good things. One dram of pride poisons many measures of grace. I will be no more afraid of doing good things amiss than of being proud when I have performed them.

26. HATRED OF SIN. It is not only commission that makes a sin. A man is guilty of all those sins which he does not hate. If I cannot avoid all sins, yet I will hate all sins.

27. PREJUDICE. Prejudice is so great an enemy to truth that it makes the mind incapable of receiving truth. In matters of faith, I will first lay a sure ground, and then I will believe, even though I cannot argue; holding the conclusion in spite of the premises. But in other lesser matters I will not so forestall my mind with resolution as to cause me to be unwilling to be better informed. Neither will I say within myself, "I will hold it, therefore it shall be true." But rather I will say, "This is truth, therefore I will hold it." I will not strive for victory, but for the truth.

28. COVETOUSNESS. Drunkenness and covetousness much resemble one another. For the more a man drinks, the more he thirsts. And the more a man has, the more he covets. As for their effects, both of them have the power to transform a man into a beast—and of all other beasts, into a swine. The former (the drunkard becoming beastly) is evident to sense, the other (the covetous becoming beastly) is more obscure, but no more

questionable. The covetous man resembles a swine in two ways. (1) in that he is forever rooting in the earth, never once looking to Heaven, (2) in that he never does any good until he does. In desiring, my rule shall be the necessity of nature, or of my estate. In having, I will esteem that my good which does me good.

29. PRAYER. I acknowledge no Master of requests in Heaven except one, Christ my Mediator. I know that I cannot be so happy as not to need Him. Nor can I be so miserable that He should condemn me. I will always ask, and that of no one but where I am sure to get what I ask, but I will ask where there is so much to give that when I have had the most, there shall be no less left to give. Though numberless drops are in the sea, yet if one is taken out of it there is less water to take (though not discernible). But God, because He is infinite, can admit of no decrease. Men are niggardly, for the more they give the less they have. But Thou, O Lord, may give what Thou wilt, without lessening Thy store. Good prayers never come weeping home. I am sure that I shall either receive what I ask, or I shall receive what I should ask.

30. LOVE. To love in order to receive a benefit is the basest love of all. For in this we are not loving another, but ourselves. Though there were no Heaven, I would love the Lord. Since there is a Heaven, I will esteem it, I will desire it—yet I will still love Thee alone, for Thy goodness sake. Thou are reward enough for me, even if Thou didst give me no more.

31. BLASPHEMY. Men will desperately endanger their lives to revenge a disgraceful word spoken against themselves. But they will be content to hear God pulled out of Heaven with blasphemy and not feel so much as a rising of their blood. This argues our cold love for God, our over-affection for ourselves. In my own wrongs I will hold patience to be laudable, but in God's injuries, I will count patience to be impious.

32. NOBILITY. There is no free man with God unless he be His servant (though he is in the galley). There is no slave except the sinner (though he is in a palace). There are no nobles except the virtuous (though never so basely descended). None are rich except he who possesses God (even if he is in rags). None are wise but he who is a fool to himself and the world. None are happy except those the world pities. Let me be free, noble, rich, happy unto God, I do not care what I am to the world.

33. PRAYER. When the mouth prays, man hears. When the heart prays, God hears. Every good prayer knocks are the door of Heaven for a blessing. But an importunate prayer pierces it and makes way for itself, into the ears of the Almighty. And as it ascends

it is carried with the wings of faith. So, as it comes down again, it is heavily loaded. In my prayers my thoughts shall not be guided by my words, but my words shall follow my thoughts.

34. TEMPTATION. Heaven is compared to a hill, so it is figured by Mt. Olympus among the heathen; by Mount Zion in God's book. Hell, on the contrary, is compared to a pit. The ascent to the one is hard, therefore, and the descent to the other is easy and head-long. So, if we once begin to fall, the recovery is most difficult. Not many stop before he comes to the bottom. I will be content to pant and gasp and sweat in climbing up to Heaven. And I will be wary of setting the first step downward towards the pit. For, as there is a Jacob's ladder into Heaven, so there are blind stairs that go winding down to death, and each step makes way for the other. The steps of temptation are these: From the object is raised an ill suggestion; suggestion draws on delight; delight brings consent; consent causes endeavor; endeavor brings practice; pract-ice soon establishes custom; custom brings excuses; excuses must have defense; defense of a bad cause invariably ends in obstinacy; obstinacy will bring boasting of sin; boasting causes a reprobate sense. I will watch over my ways, and ask the Lord to watch over me, so that I may avoid the first steps of sin. And if those over-take me in my frailty, then, "O Lord, keep me so that presumpt-uous sins do not prevail over me." Beginnings are easier and safety declined quicker when we are free, much more than when we have begun to proceed.

35. THE USE OF MEANS. Asa was only sick in his feet, far from his heart; yet he died because he sought to the physicians instead of going to God. Hezekiah was sick unto death, yet he did not die be-cause he trusted in God, not in the physicians. Means without God cannot help. God without means can help, and He often does. I will use good means, but I will not rest in them.

36. WORSHIP. An evil man is clay to God, wax to the devil. God may stamp him into powder, or He may temper him anew—but none of His means can melt him. On the contrary, a good man is God's wax and clay to Satan. He relents at every look from God, but he is not stirred by any temptation. I had rather bow to God than to be broken. But as for Satan and the world, I would rather be broken in pieces with their violence than to allow myself to be bowed unto their obedience.

37. HAPPINESS. There is no man as happy as a Christian. When he looks up to Heaven, he thinks, "That is my home; the God who made it and owns it is my Father; the angels, more glorious in nature than myself, are my attendants; my enemies are my ser-

vants." Yea, those things which are the most terrifying to the wicked are most pleasant to the Christian. When he hears God thunder above his head, he thinks, "This is the voice of My Father." When he remembers the tribunal of the last judgment, he thinks, "It is my Saviour who will sit in judgment." When he thinks of death, he esteems it but as the angels set before Paradise—which with one blow admits him to eternal joy. And (which is most of all) nothing in earth or hell can make him miserable. There is nothing in the world worth envying, that is, nothing but a Christian.

35. OBEDIENCE. Shimei, seeking his servant, left the gates of Jerusalem, thus disobeying King Solomon and losing his life by it. I see a number who, like Shimei, are seeking their servant (which is riches) and losing their souls. I shall let no worldly thing draw me outside the gates within which God has confined me.

36. REPENTANCE. I brought enough sin with me into the world to repent of during my entire life, though I should never actually sin. And I sin enough every day to sorrow for, even if I had brought none with me into the world. But, laying them both together, my time is far too short for my repentance. It would be sheer madness in me to spend my short life in jollity and pleasure, for which I have such small occasion, and at the same time neglect the opportunity for just repentance. Before I came into the world, I sinned; after I have left the world, the contagion of my sin will add to the guilt of it—yet in both these states I am not able to repent. Therefore I will repent while I may, for if I neglect it now, I shall never recover the opportunity.

37. AMBITION. Ambition is torment enough for an enemy. For it affords as much discontentment in success, as in the lack of it. Ambition makes men like poisoned rats, which, when they have tasted their bane, cannot rest until they drink—and then they are even more restless until they die. It is better for me to live in the stocks as a wise man, in a contented want, than to live in a fool's paradise, vexing myself with willful unquietness.

38. CONCEIT. It is impossible for a conceited man to be anything but a fool. For the proud opinion which he has of himself excludes all opportunity to purchase knowledge. Let a vessel be once filled with the most worthless of liquors, it will not give room to the most costly, but will cause it to spill over the side. The proud man, though he is empty of all good, yet he is full of conceit. Their conceit will not give way to something better. Many men would have been proven wise if they had not thought so much of themselves. I am empty enough to receive knowledge enough if I but think I am as bare as I am—and I need no more. O Lord, do but teach me how little I have, even nothing, and give me

no more than I know that I lack.

39. THE SHORTNESS OF LIFE. Many vegetable and many brute creatures exceed man in length of days. This has opened the mouths of heathen philosophers to accuse nature of being a stepmother to man, having given to him the least time to live, though he is the only creature who could make use of his time to get knowledge. But it is in this that religion most magnifies God in His wisdom and justice. For God teaches us that other creatures live long but perish to nothing; only man recompenses the shortness of his life with eternity after it; that the sooner he dies well, the sooner he comes to perfection of knowledged (which he might seek in vain below)—the sooner he dies ill, the less hurt he does with is knowledge. Therefore, there is great reason why man should live long, but there are greater reasons why he should die early. I will never blame God for making me happy too soon, for changing my ignorance into knowledge; my corruption for immortalitie, my infirmities for perfection. "Come Lord Jesus, come quickly!"

40. SELF-EXAMINATION. It is said of the elephant that he, being aware of his deformity, cannot abide to look upon his own face in the water. Instead, he seeks for troubled, muddy channels. This we see well moralized in men of evil conscience, who know that their souls are so filthy that they dare not so much as look upon them. For to do so calls the eye of the soul home to itself, making them see a glimpse of what they do not like to see. So I have seen a foolish and timorous patient who, though knowing that his wound is deep, would not endure the surgeon to search it (and what could happen but that there will be a festering of the part, a danger to the whole body?). So I have seen many prodigal wasters run so far in the books of their creditors that they cannot abide to hear of reckoning. It has been an old and true proverb, "oft and even reckonings make long friends." I will often sum up my estate with God so that I may know what I have to expect and answer for. Neither shall my score run on so long with God that I shall not know my debts, or until I fear an audit, or until I despair of pardon.

41. ADVERSITY. The common fears of the world are causeless and ill-placed. No one fears to do ill, but every man fears to suffer ill. But in considering this, we shall find that we fear our best friends. For, for my part, I have learned more of God and of myself in one week of extremity than all my whole life's prosperity had taught me before. Besides, in reason and common experience, we find that prosperity makes us forget our death. But, on the other hand, adversity makes us neglect our life. Now (if we measure both of these by their effects) forgetfulness of death makes

us feel secure, but neglect of this life makes us care about a better life. Therefore, as much as neglect of life is better than forgetfulness of death (and as much as watchfulness is better than security,) so much more beneficial will I esteem adversity than prosperity.

42. AFFLICTION. Some children are of such a nature that they are never well unless the rod is over them. So am I to God. Let Him beat me with the rod of affliction, just so he changes me. Let Him take all away from me, just so He gives me Himself!

43. FAITH AND PHILOSOPHY. Between the school of God and the school of nature, there are two contrary ways of proceeding. In the school of nature, we must first conceive, and then believe. In the school of God, we must first believe, and then we will conceive. He that believes no more than he conceives can never be a Christian. Nor can he that assents without reason ever be a philosopher. In nature's school, we are taught to bolt out the truth by logical discourse. But God cannot endure a logician. In His school, he who reasons least and assents most is the best scholar. In divine things, then, I will conceive what I may, the rest I will believe and admire. It is not a curious head, but a believing and simple heart that is accepted with God.

44. PLEASURE. Extremity distinguishes friends. Worldly pleasures, like physicians, give us over when we are once dying. And yet the deathbed has the most need of comfort. Christ Jesus stands by the bed of those that are His, in the very pangs of death. And after death, at the bar of Judgment, He is there, not leaving them either in their bed or in their grave. As for pleasures, I will use them to my best advantage, but I will not trust in them. But for Thee, O my Lord, who in mercy and truth cannot fail me, though Thou shouldst kill me, yet I would trust in Thee, for I have found Thee ever faithful and present in all extremities.

45. SIN. It is a fearful thing to sin, more fearful to delight in sin; it is even worse than worst to boast of it. Therefore, if I cannot avoid sin-because I am a man, yet I will avoid the delight, defense and boasting of sin—because I am a Christian.

46. FAITHFUL FRIENDS. As nothing makes such strong and mortal hostility as discord in religions, so nothing in the world unites the hearts of men so firmly as the bond of faith. There are 3 grounds of friendship: Virtue, Pleasure, Profit. And, by all confessions, the surest basis of friendship is virtue. It must of necessity follow that the friendship which is based on the best and most heavenly virtue (faith) must be the firmest of all. Faith unites man to God so inseparably that no temptations, no torments, not even the gates of hell can sever them. So it also unites one

Christian soul to another so firmly that no outward occurrences, no imperfections in the party loved, can dissolve their friendship. If I do not love the child of God (for his own sake, for his Father's sake) more than my friend (who is so because of his usefulness, or because he is a blood kinsman,) then I have never received any spark of true heavenly love.

47. SCHISM AND TRUTH. Most schisms are bred through pride (while men with a high conceit of themselves scorn to go in the common road, affecting singularity in opinion,) they are confirmed through anger (while they stomach and allow any contradiction,) and they are nourished through covetousness. In some cases, however, covetousness obtains the first place, anger the second, pride the last. For this reason I have always been inclined to commend and admire those great and profound minds who never were led into the byways, being delivered by humility and depth of knowledge. These men, walking in the beaten path of the Church, have bent all their forces to the establishment of received truths. For they esteemed it greater glory to confirm an ancient truth than to devise a new opinion (though it were never so profitable). I will not reject a truth for the sake of mere novelty. Old truths may come newly to light, neither is God tied to times for the gift of His illumination. But I will suspect a novel opinion of untruth, and I will not entertain it unless it may be deduced from ancient grounds.

48. GRIEF AND WORRY. Grief for things past, (things that cannot be remedied) and care for things to come (things that cannot be prevented) may easily hurt me—they can never benefit me. I will therefore commit myself to God in both, thus enjoying the present.

49. FEAR. The wicked man is a coward of cowards, he is afraid of everything. He is afraid of God, because he is His enemy; of Satan, because he is his tormentor. He is afraid of God's creatures, because they join with their Maker in fighting against him. He is afraid of himself, because he bears about with him his own accuser and executioner. On the contrary, the godly man is afraid of nothing. He is not afraid of God, because he knows Him to be his best friend, One who will not hurt him. He is not afraid of Satan, because he knows that he cannot hurt him; not of affliction, because he knows they come from a loving God and end in his own good. He is not afraid of the creatures, for the very stones of the field are in league with him; not of himself, for his conscience is at peace. A wicked man may feel momentarily secure, because he does not know what he has to fear; or he may feel desperate, through the extremity of fear. But a wicked man can never be truly courageous. Faithlessness cannot but choose to be false-hearted. I will,

by my courage, always be giving proof of my faith. But the more I fear, the less I will believe.

50. THE HEATHEN AND THE CHRISTIAN.

I have often been amazed (yes, and blushed for shame) to read in mere philosophers (who have no other mistress but nature) such strong resolution in contempt of fortunes. They had such notable precepts for a constancy and tranquility of mind! Comparing it with my own disposition and practice, I find myself too much drooping and dejected under small crosses; too easily carried away with a little prosperity. To see such courage and strength to condemn death in those who thought they completely perished at death, and to find such faint-heartedness in myself at the first thought of death (though I am thoroughly persuaded of the future happiness of my soul after death) makes me blush in shame. I have the benefit of nature, as well as they have. But I have infinite other helps that they lacked. O the dullness and blindness of us unworthy Christians! What a shame that we allow heathen philosophers to go further by the candlelight of nature than we go by the clear sun of the Gospel! How could an indifferent man tell by our practice which is the pagan? Let me never count myself a Christian unless my art of Christianity has matched and gone beyond nature far enough that I can find the best of the heathen as far below me as they found the vulgar sort of their day below them. Otherwise, I may shame my religion, and it will not help me.

51. THE LIGHT OF THE EYE, THE MIND, AND THE HEART.

A man of faith has three eyes. He has the eye of sense, which is common to him and brute animals. Secondly, he has the eye of reason, which is common to all men. Thirdly, he has the eye of faith, which is proper only to his profession. Each of these looks beyond the other. None of them meddles with the others' objects. For the eye of sense does not reach to intelligible things and matters of discourse. Nor does the eye of reason look to those things which are supernatural and spiritual (1 Cor. 2:14). And the eye of faith does not look down to those things which may be seen by the eye of sense or the eye of reason.

If you talk to a brute animal about the depths of philosophy, however plainly you may talk, he will not understand because they are beyond the view of his eye. If you talk to a carnal man about divine things, he does not perceive the things of God, nor indeed can he, for they are spiritually discerned (1 Cor. 2:14). So it is no wonder if those things seem unlikely and incredible, yea, impossible to him. But the faithful man having the means of apprehension plainly sees spiritual things, even as his sensible eye sees the things of matter. Tell an unlearned man that the sun or some barely seen star is much bigger than his cartwheel, or at least many times bigger than the whole earth, and he will laugh you to scorn. Yet the scholar, by the eye of reason, plainly sees and acknowledges this truth as much as that his hand is bigger than his pen.

O what a thick mist, what a palpable darkness, yea, more, what an Egyptian blackness does the natural man live in! What a world there is, that he does not see. And how little does he see in this world, which is his proper element! There is no body which the brute animals cannot see as well as man, and some of them he can see far better. As for the eye of reason, how dim it is in those things which are best fitted to it! What thing in nature does a man perfectly know? Not a vegetable, a flower or a worm that he treads on! No, not so much as what is in his own bosom: what it is, where it comes from, or who it is that gives him being. And as for the things which concern the best world, he does not so much as confusedly see them, neither does he know that they are. He does not see a whit into the great and fearful majesty of God. He does not see Him in all His creatures; he does not see him filling the world with His infinite and glorious presence. He does not see His wise providence overruling all things, disposing all events, ordering all sinful actions of men to His own glory. The natural man does not see anything of the beauty, majesty, power and mercy of the Saviour of the world, sitting in His humanity at His Father's right hand. He does not see the unspeakable happiness of the glorified saints. He does not see the whole heavenly commonwealth of angels ascending and descending to the need of God's children, waiting on him at all times invisibly. Nor does he see the multitude of invisible spirits passing him, standing by him, to tempt him to evil. But man is like the foolish bird that hides his head so that he cannot see anybody, thinking thereby that no one can see him. It was not without cause that we learned to call a fool natural-born. For (whatever worldings have thought about Christians being God's fools,) we know them to be the fools of the world. The deepest philosopher that ever existed is but an ignorant sot when compared to the simplest Christian. For the weakest Christian may see somewhat into the greatest mysteries of nature, because he has the eye of reason common with the best—but the best philosopher by all the demonstration in the world can conceive nothing of the mysteries of godliness, because he utterly lacks the eye of faith.

Though my insight into the matters of the world is so shallow that my simplicity moves others to pity, yet I shall be both content and happy because I can see further into much better matters. That which I cannot see is comparatively worthless, deserving little more than contempt; while that which I see is unspeakable, inestimable, both for comfort and for glory.

52. HEARTFELT RELIGION. There is nothing more easy than to say divinity by rote; to discourse of spiritual matters from the tongue or pen of others. But to hear God speak divine truth to the soul, to feel the power of religion in ourselves, to express it out of the truth of experience within—this is both hard and rare. In the matters of God, whatever we do not feel is but hypocrisy. Therefore, the more we profess the more we sin. It will never be well with me until I get to where I do not care about the censures of others in these greatest things, until I am fearful only of God's censures, and of my own. I shall not be happy until sound experience has really catechised my heart, making me to know God and my Saviour in some other way than merely by words. I will never be quiet until I can see and feel and taste God! I shall expect my hearing to serve only to effect this, and my speech shall only be to express it.

53. HURTING OURSELVES. There is no enemy that can hurt us, except ourselves alone. Satan could not hurt us if our own corruption did not betray us. Affliction could not hurt us without our own impatience. Temptations cannot hurt us if we do not yield to them. Death could not hurt us without the sting of our own sins. Sin could not hurt us without our own impenitence. O how I might defy all things if I could but get to where I was not my own enemy! I love myself too much, and yet I do not love myself enough. O my God and my Father, teach me to wish myself only as well as Thou dost desire me to be! Then I will be safe.

54. THE HEART AND THE TONGUE. Joy and sorrow are hard to conceal, for both the countenance and the tongue reveal it. For there is so much correspondence between the heart and the tongue that they will both move at once. That is why every man speaks of those things which give him pleasure, things of which he cares. The falconer speaks of his games, the plowman of his team, the soldier of his march and colors, etc. If the heart were as full of God, the tongue could not refrain from talking of Him. The rareness of this in the communications of Christians argues the common poverty of grace. If Christ is not in our hearts, we are godless. And if He is there without causing us joy, then we are senseless. And if we rejoice in Him, but do not speak of Him, then we are shameful and unthankful. Everyone takes occasion to speak of what he likes. And as I will always think of Thee, O Lord, so it shall be my joy to speak of Thee often. And if I do not find the opportunity to do so, I will make it.

55. THE USE OF TIME. The eldest of our long-lived forefathers only lived a day unto God, for a thousand years is as a day to Him.

And we, then, live but an hour compared to the day of our fore-fathers. For our fourscore years are but a twelfth of their 960. And yet of this hour which we have, there is scarce a minute for God? For, taking away all the time that is consumed in sleeping, dressing, eating, talking and sporting, the time that remains is not much more than nothing. Yet most people seek for pastimes to hasten the passing of the little time that is left. Those that seek to hurry the pace of time are spurring a racing horse. I have more need to redeem my time with double care and labor than to seek ways to sell it for nothing.

56. CARES. He who takes his own cares upon himself loads himself with an uneasy burden in vain. The fear of what may come, the expectation of what will come, the desire of what will not come, and the inability to adjust to all of these will necessarily breed continual torment for him. I will cast all my cares upon God, for He has told me to do it. My cares cannot hurt Him, and He can redress them.

57. PROVIDENCE. There is not the least action or event which is not overruled and disposed by Providence. This not only does not detract anything from the majesty of God, in that they are small, but there can be no greater honor to Him than to extend His providence and decree to them because they are infinite. Nor does this providential order hold only to natural things only, things which are chained to one another by a regular order of succession, but it also holds in those things which seem to happen only by accident and by imprudence. When anything happens contrary to what I have purposed, I shall be contented, knowing that God has purposed it as it happened. So, then, the thing has attained His own end, even while it was missing mine. I know what I want, but God knows what I should want. It is enough that His will is done, even if my will must be crossed.

58. LOVE. As love keeps the whole law of God, so love alone is the breaker of the law. For love is the ground of all obedience, and so it is the ground of all sin. For sin has been commonly thought to have two roots, love and fear, but it is plain that fear has its origin in love. For no man fears to lose anything except those things he loves. It is here that sin and righteousness are both brought into a short sum, both depending upon our affection. It shall be my only care, therefore, to bestow my love well, both for the object and the measure of it. All that is good, I may love. But I must love in different degrees: what is simply good, I shall love absolutely; what is good by circumstance, I shall love with limitation. There are three things which I may love without limitation: God, my neighbor, and my soul. Yet each must have its due place.

My body, my fame, my goods, etc. I shall regard as servants to God, my neighbor, and my soul. All other things I will either not care for, nor I will not hate them.

59. DISPLEASURE. God gives pleasing things to some in anger, just as He strikes some others in love. The Israelites would have fared better if they had lacked their quail than to have eaten them with the sauce of God's anger. Sometimes, at our insistence, a lesser punishment is removed from us, and a greater punishment is given in its stead (though we may be insensible of it). I will not so much strive against affliction as I do against displeasure. Let me rather be afflicted in love than to prosper without it.

60. FRIENDSHIP. When men have such continual provision from God and are so perpetually beholding to Him, is it not strange that we are such strangers to Him, so little acquainted with Him. We count it perverse in any man when he refuses the familiarity of a worthy friend who seeks and has deserved his friendship. Then why are we so loath to think of our dissolution and going to be with God? It is natural that we do not want to hazard a welcome in going where we are not acquainted, but we go boldly and willingly to the house of a dear friend with whom we have familiarly conversed for a long time. Yet we seek and scrape for an acquaintance with the world (which never did us any good) even when we have been repulsed many times. And we neither seek nor scrape for an acquaintance with God. I will not live with God, in God, without being acquainted with Him, for I know that it is my happiness to have such a friend. I will not let a single day pass without some act of renewing my familiarity with Him. Not one day shall pass without some testimony of my love being given to Him, some expression of my joy in Him being made known to Him. I will not rest until He has left behind Him some pledge of His continued favor to me.

61. BARGAIN HUNTING. In all other things, we are led by profit. But in the main matter of all, we show ourselves to be utterly unthrifty. We may be wise in making good markets in the base commodities of the world, but we show ourselves to be foolish in marketing for our souls. God and the world both make offers to us. The world, like a frank merchant, says, All these things I will give you, and it thrusts its things, its promotions, into our hands. God tells us, I will give you a crown of glory. But He asks for a day to perform this, giving us for the present but an earnest of the bargain. And though we know that there is no comparison between the two in value, finding these earthly things unable to give us any contentment, knowing those other are of invaluable worth and benefit, yet we had rather take these things of the world in hand than to trust God on His word for the future. Yea, we would take some

rich lordship on the expectation that three lives may expire in order that we may receive it, rather than to take a smaller sum of money for the present—but contrarily when it is God that is offering us future riches, we take the world's offer of painted, cheap wares. And we may buy them at such a dear price as the torment of our souls. Yet God proclaims, Come, you that lack, buy of Me without money and without price. We are supposed to be thrifty men, trying all shops in order to get the best bargain, but we refuse God, who is offering us His precious commodities for nothing. We are willing to pay a hard price for things which are worse than nothing, things which may be painful to us! Surely we are not so wise for the body as we are foolish, and we are not wise as to our souls in anything. O Lord, Thy payment is sure, and who knows how present it may be? Take the soul that Thou hast made, which Thou hast bought, and let me rather give my life for Thy favor than to take the offers of the world for nothing.

62. REPROOF. I see that iron is first heated red hot in the fire, and afterwards it is beaten and hardened with cold water. So I will deal with an offending friend. First I will heat him with deserved praise, then I will beat upon him with reproof. Good nurses, when they pick up a child that has fallen, usually speak good words to them at first, then chide them afterwards. Gentle speech is a good preparative for rigor. He shall see that I love him by my approval, and he shall see that I do not love his faults by my reproof. If he loves himself, he will love those that do not like his vices. If he does not love himself, it does not matter whether he loves me.

63. ENVY. The more we are like God, the better and happier we will be. All sins make us unlike Him, being contrary to His perfect holiness. But some sins are more directly contrary to Him, envy is one of these. For whereas God brings good out of evil, the envious man fetches evil out of good, and in this his sin also proves to be a kind of punishment. For even evil things work together for good to good men, but to the envious good things work together for evil to him. I will never envy the evil in any man, though he be ever so prosperous—I will pity him. I will not envy good graces either, but I will emulate them, rejoicing that they are so good, grieving that I am no better.

64. WORLDLY PLEASURES. Those that have tasted of some delicate dish find other things plain, even unpleasant. So it is with those who have once tasted of heavenly things, they cannot but have contempt for the very best worldly pleasures. Therefore, I will be as a guest who knows that there is much more pleasant fare to come, I will reserve my appetite for that which is to come, not

allowing myself to become satiated with the coarse food of this world.

65. FOLLOWING GOOD EXAMPLES. It is indeed more commendable to give a good example than to take one. Yet imitation of Christian practice has its due praise. However, much caution must be exercised that we follow good men, and that we follow them in that which is good. We must follow good men, for if we follow imperfect patterns then will be forced to unlearn those ill habits we have by imitating the wrong kind of man. We must follow them only in that which is good, for a man should not be so wedded to another man's person that he makes no distinction between his infirmities and his goodness. Therefore, he that would follow well must know how to distinguish between good men and evil ones, between good qualities and weaknesses. Why has God given me my education in the company of good and virtuous men, if it is not that I should better myself by watching their good carriage? The Psalmist compares the law of God to a lantern. Good example bears the lantern. It is safe following him who carries the light. If he walks without the light, then he shall walk without me.

66. TIME. There is nothing in this life that is diminished by addition—except life, itself. For every moment that is added to our lives is a minute that is deducted from our lives. It is added minute by minute, it is subtracted minute by minute—so it is not perceptible. The shorter the minutes, the more slyly they pass away from us. I shall not allow time to so steal upon me that I do not discern it. I will catch it by the forelocks, I will not allow it to so steal away from me that it carries no witness of its passage in my added proficiency in the things of God.

67. ENJOYMENT. The joy of a Christian in the things of this world must be limited, for he must be filled with fear of excess, and he must know that he can be abundantly recompensed with spiritual mirth only. But the worldling gives the reigns to his mind, pours himself out into pleasure, fearing only that he shall not have joy enough. He who is only half a Christian always lives miserably. For he neither enjoys God or the world. He does not enjoy God because he does not have grace enough to make Him his own. He does not enjoy the world because he has enough of a taste of grace to show him the emptiness, the vanity, the sin of its pleasures. So the sound Christian has his heaven above; the worldling has his 'heaven' below; the mere professor of Christianity has no heaven anywhere.

68. GOOD WORKS. Good deeds are very fruitful, not so much because they are good, but because God blesses and multiplies them. We think that 10 of 100 is extreme usury, but God give us more

than 100 for 10. For out of one good action of ours, God produces a thousand—the harvest of it is perpetual. Even the faithful acts of the old patriarchs and the constant sufferings of the ancient martyrs still live, they are still doing good to all ages by their example. Public acts of virtue, besides being presently comfortable to the doer, are also examples to others. And as they are more beneficial to others, they are the more crowned in us. Even if good deeds were barren of outward gain, I would still seek after them for the conscience of their own goodness. How much more I shall be encouraged to perform them when they are so profitable both to others and to me, and to me in others? My principle care shall be that while my soul lives in glory in Heaven, my good acts may still be living on earth. I will be glad that they have been put into the bank to multiply while my body lies in the graves and consumes.

69. FRUITFULNESS. Because of the sweet fruit he bears for God and man, a Christian is compared to the noblest of all plants, the vine. Now as the most generous vine, it it is not pruned, runs out into many superfluous stems and grows weak and fruitless—so does the best man, if he is not cut short of his desires, pruned by afflictions. If it is painful to bleed, it is worse to wither. Let me be pruned that I may grow, rather than cut up and burned.

70. FOOLISHNESS. There are three times when a wise man does not differ from a fool: In his infancy, in his sleep, and in his silence. In infancy and in sleep, we are all fools. In silence, we are all wise. Foolishness may be concealed in infancy and in sleep, but the tongue is a blabber: There cannot be any kind of foolishness (either simple or wicked) in the heart without the tongue betraying it. He who speaks much, who speaks without sense, or who speaks out of season cannot be wise. And he who says nothing cannot be known for a fool. It is a great misery to be a fool, but it is a greater misery for a man to be a fool that cannot restrain himself from showing it. It would be well for that man if he could be taught to keep his foolishness a secret—but then there would be no fools. I have heard some speak in the hope that they would show themselves witty; and I have heard them censured by those who thought themselves wiser. Still another has censured the second by lack of wisdom in censuring. Surely a man is not a fool for having unwise thoughts, but he is a fool for uttering them. Even concealed foolishness is wisdom, and sometimes it is foolish to utter wisdom. Others may be careful how they speak, but my care shall be how to keep my mouth shut.

71. DOING GOOD. A work is only good and acceptable when the act, the meaning, and the manner of it are good. For to do good while intending ill (as Judas' kiss) is as much more sinful as the act

itself is good. Though it is good in kind, it is abused to an evil purpose. To do evil with good intentions (as Uzzah did in steadying the Ark) is amiss because the good intention cannot make the unlawful act good. And though there may seem to be some excuse for doing evil with good intentions, yet there is no warrant from God to justify it. To mean well and to do good, but to do it in an ill manner (as the Pharisee prayed a good prayer, but he did it arrogantly) is so offensive that the evil manner corrupts the other. If a thing is evil in but one of the three (the act, the intention, or the way it is done), it cannot be good at all. Therefore, in whatever business I attempt, I will inquire, What shall I do, How shall I do it, and, Why do I do it. As to what I shall do and how I am to do it, I shall consult with God. As to why I am doing it, I shall consult carefully with my own heart.

72. HERMITAGE. The precepts and practices of those with whom we must live means very much. It is less commendable if a man does not evil when he has no provocations to evil, than for a man to live continently in a evil place where there is much allurement to uncleaness. It is truly praiseworthy for Lot to be a good man in the midst of Sodom. To sequester ourselves from the company of the world in order to depart from their vices comes from a base and distrusting mind. It is as if we were trying to force goodness upon ourselves, thinking that we must be good because we cannot be tempted to evil by others. But it well becomes the courage of a Christian to be personally and locally in the throng of the world and yet withdraw his affections from it; to use the world, yet to have contempt for it; to compel the world to do service to God, yet not to become infected by it. The world shall be mine, I will not belong to the world—and it shall be mine so that its evil shall still remain its own.

73. A HAPPY LIFE. If a man lives in God, then he cannot be weary of his life, because he can always find something to do and something for solace. And the godly man can never be overly sad at parting with the world, because he shall enter into a happier life and society with the God in whom he delights. But if a man lives without God, he lives many times more uncomfortably here, because he does not know any cause of joy within himself, and because he does not find anything worth doing to while away his time here. Such a man dies miserably because he either knows not where he is going, or because he knows that he is going to torment. There is no life worthy of the name except the life of faith. O Lord, let me not live in the world without Thee.

74. HEAVENLY CORRECTION. I have seen who afflicted their bodies with willful famine and with other scourges of their own

making. God spares me such labor, for He whips me daily with the scourge of a weak body, and sometimes with ill tongues. He sometimes holds me short of the feeling of His comfortable presence, which is far more miserable a hunger than that of the body (for the soul is more tender, and the food of the soul is much more excellent). But He is my Father, and He is infinitely more wise to proportion out my correction according to my need—and He is infinitely more loving in giving me the exact measure of correction that I need. That man who must choose his own rod is a presumptuous child indeed. Let me learn to make a right use of God's corrections, then I shall not need to correct myself. And if it should please God to remove His hand a little, then I will govern my body as a master—but I shall not treat it as if I were a tyrant.

75. HEAVENLY HUNGER. If God had not said, "Blessed are those that hunger," I do not know what could keep weak Christians from despair. Many times it is all that I can do to discover and complain that I do not have Him, and to wish to recover Him. This is my comfort, that He in mercy esteems not only what we have, but what we desire to have also. And in a way He counts us to have that which we lack, that which we desire to have. And my soul tells me that I unfeignedly long after that grace which I miss. O let me desire more, and I know that I shall not have to desire always. There was never a soul which miscarried by longing after grace. O blessed hunger that ends always in fullness! I am sorry that I can only hunger, yet I do not want to be full, for the blessing is promised to the hungry. O give me more, Lord, but in such a way that I still may hunger more—then I know that I shall be satisfied.

76. REPENTANCE. A wicked man carries a burning brand to his fire every day, and when his heap is at its height he ceases his sinful days and begins his torment. But a repentant man carries away a burning faggot from the flame with every fit of holy sorrow. And his tears quench the coals that remain. There is no torment for the repentant soul, and there is no redemption for the impenitent. Safety does not consist in refraining from sin, but it consists in repenting of sin. It is not sin that condemns, it is impenitence. O Lord, I cannot be righteous, make me repentant.

77. SPIRITUAL WARFARE. Our spiritual war does not allow any intermission. It knows no night, no winter; it allows no peace, no truce. In this war we are never in a garrison, where we may have rest and respite. But we are continually in the field fighting pitched battles, looking our enemy in the face, being always under assault from him. We are forever resisting, defending, receiving and returning blows. If we are ever negligent, we die. If we become weary, we die. There is hope while we fight, death if we stand still.

We can never have safety and peace except in victory. Therefore our resistance must be courageous and constant, for yielding will bring death to our cause, and treaties of peace with the enemy also.

78. STRENGTH IN TRIALS. God forewarns us before He sends trials, but Satan steals upon us suddenly by temptations (desiring to foil us). If we do not relent when God's warning comes, if we linger in the pace of punishment He sets, then He punishes much more (according to how much His warning was more evident to us). God's trials must be met when they come; Satan's must be seen before they come. If we do not arm ourselves before we are assaulted, we shall be foiled before we can take up arms.

79. HEAVENLY-MINDEDNESS. Greatness puts high thoughts and big words into a man. But the dejected mind takes whatever offers itself, seemingly not caring. Every worldling is base-minded; that is why his thoughts creep low upon the earth. The Christian is great and knows himself to be so; that is why he minds and speaks of those great spiritual, immortal, glorious, heavenly things of Christianity. As much as one's soul stoops to earthly thoughts, so much is his soul unregenerate.

80. HUMILITY. Sometimes it is well taken by men that we humble ourselves lower than there is cause. And no less well does God take these submissions of ourselves ("I am a worm and no man.") ("Surely I am more foolish than a man and have not the understanding of a man in me.) But I never find that anyone who has bragged to God and was accepted (even though it may be in a matter of truth and within the compass of his desert). A man may be too lowly in his dealings with men, even to where they are contemptuous. But with God a man cannot be too low—the lower he falls, the higher is his exaltation.

81. DEATH. Death did not first strike Adam, the first sinful man; nor did it strike Cain, the first hypocrite. But it struck Abel the innocent and righteous one. So the first soul that met death overcame death, the first soul that departed from earth went to Heaven. Death does not argue God's displeasure, but he whom God loves best dies first, while the murderer is punished with living.

82. PURPOSE IN LIFE. The lives of most men are misspent, for lack of a certain end to their actions. They are as unwise archers who shoot away their arrows at random, without a mark. They live only in the present, not directing themselves and their acts to one universal scope. So they alter their courses upon all occasions of change, never teaching any perfection. They can do nothing but continue in uncertainty and end in discomfort.

Others aim at a certain mark, but it is a wrong one. Some, though fewer, aim at the right end, but they aim amiss.

To live without one main and common purpose is idleness and folly. To live to a false end is deceit and loss. True Christian wisdom both shows the end and finds the way. And as cunning politicians have many plots to bring about one end the same design by a planned succession, so the wise Christian must do. For even if he fails in the use of one means, he can still fetch about to his purposed end with a constant change of endeavors. Such men are the only ones to live lives of purpose, who at last do not repent that they have lived.

83. GOOD FROM EVIL. God fetches good out of evil. So may we turn our own and others' sins to both private and public good. We may not do evil for a good use, but we must use our evil, once done, to our good. I hope I shall not offend when I say that the good use which is made of sins is as gainful to God as that which arises from good actions. Happy is that man that can use either his good well, or who can get good from his evil.

84. MADNESS. That is a rare man who has no madness reigning in him. One has the dull madness of melancholy, another the conceited madness of pride. Another has the superstitious madness of false devotion, a fourth of ambition, or covetousness. A fifth has the furious madness of anger, a sixth the laughing madness of extreme mirth, a seventh a drunken madness. There is the madness of outragious lust, of curiosity, of profaneness and atheism. It is hard to count up all the kinds of madnesses in men, as it is to count their dispositions. Some are more noted and punished than others. Mad men of one kind condemn madmen of another kind, just as the sober man condemns them. Only that man is good, wise, and happy who is free from all kinds of frenzy.

85. THE PRACTICE OF MEDITATION. Lack of use causes disability, lack of habit loses perfection. Those who are not used to praying in their closet cannot pray in public (except coldly and formally). He who discontinues meditation shall be long in recovering the art. But a man who is used to these exercises (who is not dressed until he has prayed, who has not supped until he has meditated) does both these things well, and with ease. He that intermits good duties will incur a double loss: the blessing that follows good will be lost; the faculty of doing good will be lost.

Weak stomachs which cannot digest large meals must feed often. As for our souls, what we lack in measure, we must supply in frequence. We can never fully enough comprehend in our thoughts the joyfulness of Heaven, the meritorious sufferings of Christ, the terrors of death, etc. That is why we must meditate of them often.